ET 12956 9

Black Economic Development

Black Economic Development

Flournoy A. Coles, Jr.

 Nelson Hall, Chicago

Copyright © 1975 by Flournoy A. Coles, Jr.

All rights reserved. No part of this work covered by the copyrights hereon may be reproduced or used in any other form or by any means—graphic, electronic, or mechanical, including photocopying, recording, taping, or information storage and retrieval systems—without written permission of the publisher. For information address Nelson-Hall Inc., Publishers, 325 W. Jackson Blvd., Chicago, Illinois 60606.

Manufactured in the United States of America.

Library of Congress Cataloging in Publication Data
Coles, Flournoy A 1915–
  Black economic development.

  Includes bibliographical references and index.
  1. Negroes—Economic conditions. 2. Negro businessmen—United States. 3. Minority business enterprises—United States. I. Title.
E185.8.C74   338'.04'0973   74–30495
ISBN 0-88229-176-9

To Toby, Lynn and Gyasi

Contents

	Preface	ix
1.	Fundamentals of Economic Development	1
2.	Economics of Black America	13
3.	Obstacles to Black Economic Development	37
4.	Black Economic Development	61
5.	Black Business Development	101
6.	Prospects and New Approach	132

Appendixes

A.	Federal Government Programs for Black Entrepreneurs	167
B.	Private Programs for Black Entrepreneurs	177
C.	Blacks in Nixon Administration, 1974	183
	Notes	195
	Index	219

Preface

There is general agreement that the United States of America has attained the highest stage of economic development to become the richest nation in recorded history. And, yet, there remain subcommunities which are markedly underdeveloped when compared with the rest of the country, and in which the most abject poverty is everywhere visible. These pockets of underdevelopment and poverty were spotlighted, and apparently brought to the attention of many Americans for the first time, by Michael Harrington's *The Other America*.

One of the subcommunities which has not kept pace with the economic progress of the country as a whole—and which, in many important respects, that progress has bypassed—is the black community. Blacks are not only the largest minority group in the United States, but they constitute a population that is larger than that of all but twenty-four countries in the world (1969). As measured by every known economic indicator, the black population lags behind—and, in some instances, deplorably so—the standard of living enjoyed by the average American.

In the years since the end of World War II, and especially since the early 1960s, the economic status of the black community has attracted increasing interest of economists, sociologists, and other social scientists, as well as politicians, elected officials, and public servants. As a result of this increased interest, numerous proposals have been made for helping blacks to achieve a more meaningful and rewarding lifestyle, to make contributions to the productive processes of the economy, and to share more equitably in the results of those processes. Many of these proposals have been translated into action programs, at least in part. The economic status of blacks, however, has remained virtually unchanged in comparison with national averages and the majority society. Obviously, the programs—in design, implementation, or both—have been inadequate in terms of announced objectives.

This book constitutes another set of suggestions for moving the black community forward economically. To some extent, it builds on the successes and failures of previous proposals and programs. It contains, however, some new proposals—as well as old proposals with different orientations and thrusts—which together the author considers to be a unified, feasible, and realistic approach to black economic development.

This book owes its existence to many, many people. Of particular importance have been those colleagues and others who have studied and written in fields directly and indirectly related to the concerns of the book. These are noted in footnotes throughout the book, but the author wishes to take advantage of this opportunity to express his deep appreciation for the stimulation, inspiration, and information provided.

Expressions of most grateful appreciation are due to the secretarial staff of the Graduate School of Management, Vanderbilt University. Especially singled out are Miss Karen Brooks, who gave untiringly and unselfishly of her time in the typing and retyping of the manuscript, and Mrs. Diane Sullivan, who arranged the school's total workload among the secretaries in such a manner that Karen could devote a maximum amount of her time to the preparation of the manuscript.

Chapter One

Fundamentals of Economic Development

Economic development—stripped of the polemics with which economists, politicians, and policy-makers are wont to embellish it—is the process by which the adaptive capacity of an economic system or subsystem is increased. This definition, however, tends to obscure the wide-ranging controversy and disagreement among economists (and others) on the meaning and nature of economic development, and on the most efficient means to attain it.[1] It seems important, therefore, to develop a point of departure for a discussion of black economic development.

INTERPRETATIONS OF ECONOMIC DEVELOPMENT

The process of economic development implies that something is happening in, and to, an economy or a subeconomy thereof. The assumption is that that which is happening is desirable, good, beneficial or salutary—that the economy or subeconomy is undergoing changes for the better. Hence, economic development is often viewed from the vantage point of its opposite, i.e., underdeveloped or undeveloped. The words "underdeveloped" and "undeveloped" are variously interpreted by economists and others who are interested in the unique problems of societies or subsocieties generally categorized with these terms. First, they are often used to designate societies or subsocieties in which per capita income is only a fraction—say, 25 percent or less—of that which obtains in a developed society or subsociety; the difficulty with this definition is that a relatively low per capita income may still exist in a situation where development may have progressed to the point of maximum realization of economic potential in terms of available resources.

Second, the terms are used to designate societies or subsocieties in which the government considers development a problem requiring immediate and effective action. This definition is completely inadequate for analytical purposes, since it precludes situations in which the government and people are not—or, at least, do not seem to be—particularly disturbed about their development status.

Third, others would consider levels of civilization, culture, and spiritual values as important criteria for drawing a line of demarcation between developed, underdeveloped, or undeveloped. This definition could, conceivably, rank the United States and some of the other more technologically advanced nations of Europe considerably below some of the countries of Africa, Asia, and Latin America.

Fourth, to some, the terms are meant to designate those areas or countries which haven't yet become industrialized but are engaged in activities designed to achieve industrialization. This definition, obviously, would exclude those areas or countries not having resources for industrialization. Further, it assumes an a priori equality between economic development and industrialization, which may not always be tenable.

Fifth, an area or a country is often described as underdeveloped if it has a low ratio of population to land area. This interpretation suffers from the fact that a country may have certain empty spaces which are not in any one's conceivable interest to populate.

Sixth, scarcity of capital is often used as a means of characterizing an area or country as undeveloped. A scarcity of capital may be the result of either controls on the mobility of capital even though all other conditions for, say, the importation of capital may exist, a scarcity of economically justifiable and feasible investment opportunities, or a lack of quantity or quality of other factors of production to assure the most economic utilization of capital.

Seventh, there is a tendency by some to identify underdeveloped with young, with the date of settlement by people of European stock being taken as the criterion of age. Such an interpretation would, for example, make it difficult to reconcile the fact that Brazil, while older than the United States, is less economically developed, and also to explain why so many non-European countries which were not Europeanized until the late nineteenth century now have among the highest per capita incomes in the world (e.g., Japan, Australia, New Zealand).

Eighth, undeveloped or underdeveloped is sometimes identified with the failure, given a level of technological knowledge, to utilize fully the potential economic output made possible by that knowledge because of institutional obstacles. The difficulty here is that no country utilizes its productive potential to the maximum. Hence, according to this interpretation, all countries are either undeveloped or underdeveloped.

Ninth, there is the tendency to compare countries or areas on the basis of levels and characters of economic performance, and to label as "backward" countries whose economic performance is below that of other countries. Undeveloped or underdeveloped, in this sense, would apply to all but a relatively few countries of the world.

At least two other interpretations succeed in avoiding

the above inadequacies and confusion. The first is that of Jacob Viner—one of America's foremost economists, who was a professor, successively, at the University of Chicago, Princeton and Harvard—who suggests that "a more useful definition of an underdeveloped area or country is one which has good potential prospects for using more capital or more labor or more available natural resources, or all of these, to support its present population on a higher level of living, or, if its per capita income level is already fairly high, to support a larger population on a not lower level of living."[2] This puts the emphasis on existing per capita levels of living in relation to potential per capita levels of living, as a measure of development.

The second is related to Walter Rostow's stages of economic growth.[3] By this definition or criterion, a society or subsociety is economically undeveloped when it has not reached the stage in its development of "take-off into self-sustained growth," or when there have not been sufficient and adequate transformations in the economy—or society of which it is a part—for economic growth to become automatic. The take-off is a function of several factors, including rate of investment, changes in productive techniques, disposition of income flow, diversity of economic activity, existence or emergence of a conducive overall environment, level and success of entrepreneurship, and economic growth rates in particular sectors.

THE NATURE OF ECONOMIC DEVELOPMENT

The process by which the adaptive capacity of an economic system or subsystem is increased has many attributes.

First, it is an economic process, but it is more than that. Although it involves the accumulation of capital in new physical forms, changes in the techniques of production, changes in trade and consumption patterns, with consequent modifications in the old patterns of prices, occupations, incomes, it also is influenced by and is dependent upon a whole series of political, cultural, psychological, social, and other noneconomic factors and developments. On balance, and within the context of the interrelatedness between the economic and the noneconomic, successful economic development becomes a function of the extent to which (1) there is consonance between, and integration of, the various organisms which make up the total socioeconomic system, and (2) the total socioeconomic system constitutes an institutional environment which is conducive to, and promotive of, continuing economic development.

Second, economic development is a dynamic process—a dynamism which can be (and historically has been) either evolutionary or revolutionary in character. The dynamic nature of economic development refers to the changes which occur in the many variables of an economy, as a result of what Joseph A. Schumpeter in *The Theory of Economic Development* refers to as "disturbances in the routine of the circular flow in static and stationary general equilibrium."[4] An example will illustrate the point. A generally accepted measure of economic development, in both the short and long term, is the annual average rate of increase in per capita national income. This rate of increase, however, is a function of many ever-changing phenomena, including (1) increases in productivity which, in turn, are related to changes in the sizes of operations and markets, changes in the process of specialization, changing quantities of capital per unit of other productive factors, the technical and economic adaptabilities of people, and so forth; (2) technological progress; (3) improvements in the quality of the labor force; (4) monetary, fiscal, and other economic policies and programs; (5) income distribution patterns; and (6) a miscellany of noneconomic factors (e.g., religious traditions, political institutions, and ideologies, the degree of free participation by all members of society in social and economic activities).

Third, economic development is relative. In this sense, comparisons are usually made between the stages of development of two societies at a given point in time. The yardstick generally used is annual average or per capita income. Such comparisons reveal that only about one-tenth of the human race averages an income of $1000 and above per year. That this is not a completely reliable yardstick is underscored, however, when comparisons show that the per capita income of oil rich but economically underdeveloped Kuwait, in 1965, was greater than that of the United States (i.e., $4786 v. $3536).[5] Another comparison is made between the stages of development of a given society at different points in time. Presumably, this comparison measures the progress of economic development with respect to a given society over time, but there are pitfalls to be avoided in arriving at conclusions. For example, the increase in per capita income between 1960 and 1965 of 13.4 percent for Ethiopia, 69.5 percent for Israel, 12.7 percent for Brazil, and of 25.5 percent for the United States does not necessarily mean that these were the rates of economic development in these countries during that period.[6] These increases in per capita incomes say absolutely nothing about structural or qualitative changes in these countries in the 1960–1965 period; these changes, to be discussed shortly, are absolutely essential for economic development. Finally, there is the comparison between the stage of development of a given society at a given point in time and its economic potential at that same point in time. This comparison is perhaps more meaningful, but caution is also necessary in its use and application. For example, if the economic potential of Country A is 100 and it has realized 80 percent of its potential, does this mean that Country A is more developed than Country B with an economic potential of 500 but which has realized only 50 percent of that potential?

Fourth, economic development is cumulative and

progressive—i.e., current development is possible because of preceding development. To quote Joseph Schumpeter, "Every process of development creates the prerequisites for the following. Thereby the form of the latter is altered, and things will turn out differently from what they would have been if every concrete phase of development had been compelled first to create its own conditions."[7] Examples are not lacking to illustrate the cumulative and progressive nature of economic development—the progressions (1) from barter to monetary to credit economies; (2) from local to regional to national to international economies; (3) from primary to secondary to tertiary production;[8] (4) from ancient slavery to feudalism to market capitalism to industrial capitalism to socialism (and, possibly, to communism;[9] (5) from a young and growing debtor nation to a mature debtor nation to a new creditor nation to a mature creditor nation;[10] and (6) the progression from a traditional economy to a transitional economy to one at the stage of take-off into sustained economic growth and industrialization to an economy driving toward industrial maturity to a mature economy.[11] The history of the economic development of today's most advanced and most industrialized nations reveals conformity to most of these progressions—and that which is common to all these nations and the progressions which they experienced is successive additions to previous stages of development.

Fifth, related to the cumulative and progressive nature of economics is its self-reinforcing nature. As an economy goes through various stages, new targets or goals emerge and the economy, as a consequence, is under continuing pressure to advance even further along the economic development continuum. To slow the development process down—to say nothing of attempts to turn the clock back—is to court the serious dangers of economic stagnation, deterioration, and disintegration. The self-reinforcing nature of economic development is a function of both consumption (demand) and production (supply). With respect to consumption, the force is the rising expectations of people in an economy which is progressing or developing—the tendency of demand to increase and to diversify as the means of satisfying demand increase. On the production side, the force is the ability and necessity to multiply or transform factors of production, or both. For example, during the early stages of an economy's development, factor multiplication—in the form of a more intensive utilization of the more abundant productive factor (usually labor)—occurs, but without any significant alterations in production techniques as compared with the predevelopment period; in the succeeding stage, development is accelerated by an ever-increasing use of capital and by the increasing mechanization of productive processes formerly accomplished by human labor (i.e., factor transformation); and, at a more advanced stage of development, an increasing proportion of the labor force is employed in tertiary or service activities, involving both factor-multiplication (especially capital) and factor-transformation. Thus, economic development at each stage not only produces the means for progression to the next stage but the conditions which result in ultimate pressure for progression to the next stage are also created.

Sixth, the economic development process is one of constant interruptions. It is a distinct phenomenon, as Schumpeter says, of "spontaneous and discontinuous change in the channels of the (circular) flow, disturbance of equilibrium, which forever alters and displaces the equilibrium state previously existing."[12] This spontaneous and discontinuous change occurs in the industrial and commercial sectors of the economy, rather than in the consumer sector, mainly because of new combinations of production.[13] Although self-sustaining elements (expanding markets, capital accumulation, innovation, and technological change) are essential for economic development, their presence in an economy cannot guarantee uninterrupted or sustained economic progress because the growth process has built within it certain self-limiting elements. Simon Kuznets in his *Six Lectures on Economic Growth* stresses at least four of these elements: (1) scarcity of resources; (2) diminishing returns; (3) the reduction of economic incentives as incomes rise above a certain point; and (4) the strengthening of vested interests which may resist development in competitive areas of the economy.[14] In addition to these, of course, there are the familiar cyclical fluctuations or business cycles. Forced draft economic development—characteristic of totalitarian regimes and, to a different degree, of modern Israel—may mitigate the impact of some of these elements on development, but it can never completely eliminate their ultimate influence.

ECONOMIC DEVELOPMENT V. GROWTH

There is a tendency to treat synonymously the terms "economic development" and "economic growth." As has been forcefully argued by Schumpeter, among others, there are significant distinctions to be made between the two.[15] The concept of economic development involves spontaneous and discontinuous qualitative changes in economic life—changes in the framework of the economy which fundamentally displace the old equilibrium and create new and different conditions. These changes come from within a system—they are not forced upon the system from without, in the sense that they are not merely adaptations to external changes. "Should it turn out that there is no such change arising in the economic sphere itself, and that the phenomenon that we call economic development is in practice simply founded upon the fact that the data change and that the economy continuously adapts itself to them, then we should say that there is *no* economic development."[16] The changes on which economic development depends usually consist of new combinations of the factors of production or a new relationship between resources and technology. As a consequence thereof, there are new or different quality goods or services, new methods of production, the opening up of new markets, the exploitation of new sources of supply of raw materials or semi-manufactured goods, and/or the implementation of new organizations for productive purposes. Economic growth, on the other hand, involves merely increases in existing data—for example, increases in income, wealth, savings, population, etc.—without any qualitative changes being effected. Thus, although economic development is usually accompanied by economic growth, it is possible to have growth without development.

The qualitative changes in economic life imply not only new combinations between resources and technology but also concomitant changes in the social relations of production such as property, exchange, distribution, and consumption. Together these constitute the economic structure of society. Superimposed on this economic structure is a noneconomic superstructure which includes institutions and relations other than those embodied in the economic structure—such as family, law, politics, religion—plus all economic and noneconomic ideas, theories, and philosophies. It has been rather convincingly argued that the historical line of causation runs from structure to superstructure—i.e., the structure is the main cause of changes in the superstructure, or the noneconomic institutions and ideas reflect the underlying economic conditions of society.[17] This argument does not deny the possibility, however, that changes in the noneconomic superstructure can have at least indirect effects on the economic structure. Put differently—and this has important implications for black economic development—although changes in the economic structure may *ultimately* be determining elements, they are not the *only* determining elements. Changes in the superstructure can result in changes in the underlying structure.

Fundamentals of Economic Development

BLACK ECONOMIC DEVELOPMENT

Most, indeed if not all, of the above would be applicable to the black economy if one condition were present—if the black economy were not part of a total economy generally considered to be the most advanced the world has ever known. To be sure, the pervasive color-caste system of the United States (1) has created a black enclave so circumscribed and proscribed by customs and practices, often reinforced by the legal system, that its inferiority to the greater society is assured, (2) has isolated and, to a very considerable degree, insulated that enclave and its economy almost completely from the major community and its economy, and (3) has made certain that the residents of that enclave will contribute maximally to the development and maintenance of, but not participate equitably in, the benefits from the affluence of the larger economy and society. The fact remains, however, that the black economy is part of the national economy—and that what happens in and to the national economy has implications for the black economy and vice versa.

It is recognized, of course, that there is not complete agreement with this view of the black economy as an integral —not integrated—part of the national economy. One opposing view is particularly significant in terms of the major thrust of this book. This view suggests that the black economy is essentially the same as that of an underdeveloped country, and that the same principles and practices of development and developmental assistance are applicable. Indeed—as succeeding chapters will underscore—many of the characteristics usually associated with a developing country are to be found in the black economy. There are, nevertheless, differences between the black economy and those nations of the third world that are significant enough to represent almost insoluble difficulties in any attempt to treat the black economy as separate and apart from the national economy. For example, the developing countries are sovereign nations with constituted governments, echelons and channels of authority, and established spheres of accountability and responsibility. There are yet other important differences—e.g., investment opportunities, production-factor proportions, capital accumulation potentials, industrialization possibilities, the impact of technological change, labor-force characteristics, legal rights and sanctions—that are equally insoluble.

Black economic development—as is true of any other economic development—must come from within; it is dependent upon qualitative changes in the structure and processes of the black economy. It is also dependent upon, and limited by, its external environment—the national economy. Thus, black economic development programs and efforts must be directed toward effecting necessary changes within both the black economy and the national economy of which it is a part.

Chapter Two

Economics of Black America

The black population of the United States in 1971 was officially estimated at 23 million. (The actual black population is undoubtedly higher, because of the number of blacks who "pass" as whites and as other nonblacks, and because of errors and inadequacies in the gathering of data.) The official 1971 estimate represents an increase of 1.9 percent over 1970 (as compared with 1.2 percent for the total population and 2.2 percent for the total nonwhite population), and an increase of 21.7 percent over the 1960 estimate (as compared with 14.5 percent for the total population and 26.3 percent for the total nonwhite population). The black population was 11 percent of the total population throughout the 1960s and into 1971. Between 1960 and 1970, the number of black people living in the South decreased from 60 percent (of total black population) to 53 percent; the number of blacks living in metropolitan areas increased by 32.3 percent to 16.8 million, with the number of blacks living in metropolitan areas as a percentage of the total black population remaining constant at 78.3 percent.[1]

The concern of this chapter is to assess the economic status of the officially estimated 23 million minority-group people in the total population. This assessment will indicate the directions black economic development efforts must take and the magnitude of the problems it must correct.

INCOME AND POVERTY

The median income of black (and other nonwhite) families expressed as a percentage of the white median family income was 64 percent in 1970, and 54 percent in 1950.[2] During this period, however, there were fluctuations in the percentage which followed very closely fluctuations in the business cycle—rising during upturns (e.g., the Korean War of 1950–1953, the postwar capital goods boom of 1955–1957, the tax-cut boom of 1964–1965) and falling during downturns (the lowest point, 51 percent, was reached during the recession of 1958). This close correspondence suggests a high degree of sensitivity of nonwhite family income to changes in the business cycle which appears to substantiate the fact that the backwash effects of economic progress and prosperity do not apply to blacks and other nonwhites. That this is more than appearances—that advances in median income will not, in the predictable future, meet with diminishing returns in reducing the number of nonwhites below some fixed poverty-level income—is suggested by a closer look at the income data.

First, despite the narrowing of the relative differences between nonwhite and white family income during the period, the dollar gap between the two levels widened. For example, in 1950, the median income for nonwhite families was $3014 as compared with $5601 for white families, or a gap of $2387; in 1970, the median incomes were $6516 and $10,236 respectively, or a gap of $3720—widening by $1,-133.[3]

Second, the number of nonwhites in poverty is so disproportionately large that, although some may be incapable (physically or mentally) of earning livelihoods, certainly not all "are victims of specific disabilities which insulate them from the national economic climate,"[4] in terms of gainful income-producing activities. Although substantial progress was made during the period in reducing the incidence of poverty among nonwhites, about one-fifth of all nonwhite families in 1970 were receiving an annual income of less than $3000—as compared with about one-twelfth of white families. With specific reference to blacks, they accounted for about one-third of all persons below the poverty income level in 1970, for almost one-third of the family heads below this level, and for almost two-fifths of all children under eighteen in poverty-income families. More than one-half of all poor blacks lived in metropolitan areas and about two-fifths lived in the inner cities.[5]

A more specific definition of the black poor is possible. In addition to numbers of children under eighteen, black poverty occurs for the most part among (a) families headed by females (54 percent of all such black families were in poverty in 1970; but only 25 percent of white female-headed families); (b) families with male heads of household with less than eight years of completed education accounted for 60 percent of such poverty families in 1969 (as compared with 37 percent for corresponding white families); (c) families headed by employed males who earn low incomes (in 1969, these families accounted for 58 percent of the poor nonwhite families with male heads, as compared with 50 percent for similar white families); and (d) members of larger-than-average-sized families (in 1969, the average black family in poverty consisted of 4.8 persons, as compared with the national average of poor families of 3.9 and with the average poor white family of 3.6).[6] Other concentrations of nonwhite poverty are to be found among the elderly (in 1968, 46.6 percent of all elderly nonwhites as a whole, and 35 percent of the nonwhite elderly lived in metropolitan areas), also in families headed by disabled males under sixty-five.[7]

A major cause of the low-income (and poverty) status of blacks is racial discrimination, of course. The market economy of competitive private enterprise, if it worked perfectly, would be color-blind in terms of the resources utilized in the production of goods and services. To function perfectly, such a system would be characterized by equal access to education and training by those who could use them most productively, the availability of capital goods to those who could put them to the best use, equality of knowledge about work opportunities throughout the labor force, and complete mobility within the labor force into the most productive jobs. In such a system, rewards for labor expended would be based solely on contributions to the final array of goods and services available in the marketplace. To be sure, there would be some wage differentials, but they would be the result of differences in the preparation for production income—differences in education, skills, motivation, and job attitudes which make some people more productive than others. In our society, however, customs, prejudices, inertia, and (even) legislation interfere with the free functioning of the system, in terms not only of what jobs nonwhites may hold—but also what pay they should receive vis-à-vis whites similarly employed. Thus, in our society, wage income is affected more often than not by what Alan B. Batchelder in *The Economics of Poverty* describes as the authoritarian principle, by which the elite gets the lion's share of output and the remainder is distributed on the basis of status.[8] In such a situation, it has been consistently true that nonwhites, who are regarded by the white majority as inferior and less worthy, receive less than whites. For blacks, the pattern began during slavery, was further nurtured during postslavery sharecropping, and, in more recent times, has had the sanction of labor unions and governments—federal, state, and local.

EMPLOYMENT

The major source of income for blacks and other nonwhites, since they own little or no factors of production other than their own labor power, is employment. Much of this employment is low-level or low-paying in nature. Moreover, nonwhite employment is much more precarious than white employment, as indicated by differentials in unemployment rates.[9]

In 1971, nonwhites accounted for 10.9 percent of the labor force, but accounted for 18.4 percent of the unemployed. The nonwhite unemployment rate in that year was 9.9 percent, as compared with a national unemployment rate of 5.9 percent and a white unemployment rate of 5.5 percent. The highest nonwhite unemployment rate was to be found in urban poverty neighborhoods or the inner cities (12.4 percent) and the lowest was on farms (6.2 percent).[10]

A major reason for the higher unemployment rate is the familiar "last-hired-first-fired" phenomenon. The economic justification in a market economy such as ours is to be found in marginal analysis—i.e., if the marginal cost of employing labor is greater than its marginal product, the labor will not be employed. Minority or nonwhite labor tends to be high-cost labor because of its relatively low marginal product, which, in turn, is the consequence of relatively low levels of education, skills, and work experience. These relatively low levels of desirable job attributes, however, are largely the result of past and present discrimination in educational and employment opportunities.

In addition to the disproportionately high unemployment rate, the manner in which employed manpower is utilized has important implications for economic development. In this connection, one of the indications of economic progressiveness is a shift in the distribution of the labor force as related to the successive predominance in output of secondary and then tertiary industries over primary industry.[11]

Fundamental changes in the distribution of the country's overall labor forces have occurred in the post-World War II period, as indicated in Table 1.[12]

TABLE 1

Changes in Labor Force Distribution, 1950-1970

Industry Division	1950	1955	1960	1965	1970
Agriculture	7.16%	6.45%	5.46%	4.36%	3.46%
Manufacturing	15.24	16.88	16.80	18.06	19.35
Mining	0.90	0.79	0.71	0.63	0.62
Construction	2.33	2.80	2.89	3.19	3.38
Transportation and Public Utilities	4.03	4.14	4.00	4.04	4.49
Trade	9.39	10.54	11.39	12.72	14.91
Finance, Insurance and Real Estate	1.92	2.34	2.67	3.02	3.69
Service	5.38	6.27	7.42	9.09	11.61
Government	6.03	6.91	8.35	10.07	12.54
Total (a)	52.38%	57.13%	59.69%	65.18%	74.05%

(a) Totals do not include self-employed, unpaid family, and domestic service workers.

Corresponding changes in the nonwhite labor force, however, have been far less notable, as shown in Table 2 on nonwhites as a percentage of all workers in selected occupations for 1960 and 1970.[13]

In 1970, as before, there was a concentration of nonwhite workers in the low-paying service and farm occupations, as shown in Table 3.[14]

The concentration of nonwhites in the low-paying jobs is not entirely the result of low-level education, skills, and work experience. In many instances, racial discrimination rears its ugly head and becomes the primary causal factor. At every educational level, the proportion of nonwhite workers in the more attractive occupations is considerably less than the proportion of whites in such occupations.[15] Among high school graduates, 65 percent of white males have the skilled, clerical, better-paying jobs, but only 35 percent of nonwhite

TABLE 2

Nonwhites as Percentage of All Workers, 1960, 1970

Occupation	1960	1970
Total, employed	11%	11%
Professional and technical	4	7
Medical and other health,	4	8
teachers, except college	7	10
Managers, officials and proprietors	3	4
Clerical	5	8
Sales	2	4
Craftsmen and foremen	5	7
Construction craftsmen	7	7
Metal craftsmen	4	6
Foremen	2	5
Operatives	12	14
Nonfarm laborers	27	23
Private household workers	50	42
Other service workers	20	19
Farmers and farm workers	16	11

TABLE 3

Nonwhites Concentrated in Low-Paying Jobs, 1970

Occupation	Nonwhite Male	Nonwhite Female	White Male	White Female
Professional, technical and managerial	13%	13%	30%	20%
Clerical and sales	9	23	13	44
Craftsmen and foremen	14	1	21	1
Operatives	28	18	19	14
Nonhousehold service workers	13	26	6	15
Private household workers	–	18	–	3
Nonfarm laborers	18	1	6	–
Farmers and farm workers	6	2	5	2
Total	100%	100%	100%	100%

males are thus employed. Among college graduates, about 20 percent of nonwhite males are to be found in blue-collar or service work, contrasted with only 10 percent of whites. The proportion of nonwhite male college graduates in clerical work and the professions is greater than that of white male college graduates, but the proportion of nonwhite males in managerial and sales jobs is much less than that for white males. Similar patterns are observable in the employment of women; for example, approximately 40 percent of nonwhite female high school graduates and 66 percent of the elementary school graduates are in service work, yet only 12 percent and 29 percent, respectively, of white women are similarly employed. These employment differentials are observable no matter what geographical region of the country is involved. If the better-paying jobs are not actually reserved for whites, job specifications are usually so overdrawn that past discrimination in education and employment opportunities serves to disqualify most nonwhites for these jobs.

The federal government—into whose hands the rights and privileges of *all* citizens are entrusted—is among the major discriminators in employment. For example, although blacks hold almost 20 percent of all federal jobs, over 90 percent of these jobs are clustered in grades below GS–9 or its equivalent, that is, jobs paying less than $12,167 annually. In civil service jobs falling under the Classification Act, in 1970, blacks held 5 percent (318) in grades GS–9 to GS–11; 3 percent (293) in grades GS–11 to GS–19; in the Postal Field Service jobs, blacks held 7 percent (24) in PFS–9 to PFS–11; and 4 percent (8) in PFS–12 to PFS–21; and, according to wage systems, blacks held 9 percent (264) of the jobs paying $9000 and above.[16] As of April 1974, there were no cabinet officers (there has been only one in the history of the country) and only thirteen subcabinet appointments (i.e., assistant secretaries of departments); moreover, a significant percentage of blacks in high-level jobs is not to be found in positions of real decision-making but in positions which relate to the employment of other nonwhites (e.g., offices of equal opportunity), similar to vice-presidents for urban affairs, special markets, or like positions in the private sector.[17]

There is a strong and direct relationship between higher

rates of unemployment for nonwhites and overconcentration of nonwhite workers in the low-paying, unskilled, and menial occupations, on the one hand, and the relatively lower rates of labor-force participation, on the other. Whatever the degree of motivation and however strong the belief in the work ethic, it is reasonable to assume that these American values can be effectively and permanently eroded if some groups cannot find employment or can only find employment at poverty-level wages. It is, therefore, not surprising that labor-force participation rates for nonwhite males are lower in every age group than for whites. Also, the lower employment rates for nonwhite males are, of course, causally related to another fact—labor-force participation rates for nonwhite females over twenty-five years of age are higher than those for white females (see Table 4).

TABLE 4

Labor-Force Participation—1970

Age	Males		Females	
	Nonwhite	White	Nonwhite	White
Total, 16 and over	78%	81%	50%	43%
16–17 years	35	49	24	37
18–19 years	65	71	45	55
20–24 years	86	87	58	58
25–34 years	94	97	58	43
35–44 years	94	97	60	50
45–54 years	88	95	60	54
55–64 years	79	83	47	43
65 years and over	27	27	12	10

These data suggest possibly significant conclusions: (a) in the 20–44 age group, nonwhite males are only slightly less likely to be in the labor force than white males, a difference which might disappear altogether in the absence of racial discrimination; (b) the wide disparities in rates between nonwhite and white teen-age boys may indicate an early sense of defeatism and alienation on the part of the nonwhites—

with frightening sociopsychological and economic implications for the future—especially since, as will be shown in the next section, the nonwhite school enrollment percentage of this male age group is less than that for whites; (c) the lower participation rates for nonwhite men of 45–64 are causally related to the higher incidence of poverty among nonwhite families with able but unemployed male heads, with economic, social, and psychological consequences for both the present and the future; and (d) the lower participation rates of nonwhite female teen-agers, when combined with their higher than white high-school dropout rates, are probably causally related to such social concerns as prostitution, drug abuse, and illegitimacy;[19] moreover, the higher employment rates for nonwhite females of twenty-five years and above reflect the larger and increasing numbers of nonwhite families headed by women[20]:

TABLE 5

Percentage of Families Headed by Females, 1950–1970

Year	Nonwhite	White
1950	17.6%	8.5%
1955	20.7	9.0
1960	22.4	8.7
1965	23.7	8.9
1970	26.8	9.1

Furthermore, the higher employment rates for nonwhite females reflect the greater necessity for the nonwhite married woman to work to supplement the incme of the male head so that the family may have an adequate income:[21]

James Tobin, the Yale economist, argues for a tight labor market combined with national prosperity and economic growth, as a sine qua non for increased and improved black— and, this writer presumes, other nonwhite—employment and economic well-being.[23] One can agree completely with the thesis of this eminent scholar and still question the possi-

TABLE 6
Family Earners and Income, 1969

Black	No earners	One earner	Two earners	Three earners	Four or more earners
Percent of families	11%	32%	42%	10%	5%
Median income	$2162	$4416	$7782	$9027	$11,259
White					
Percent of families	8%	38%	39%	10%	4%
Median income	$3183	$8450	$10,885	$13,978	$16,243

bility of achieving such goals. Given the current problems of the economy—soaring inflation, the balance of payments, the energy crisis—and an obvious lack of commitment on the part of government toward the achievement of these objectives, it is difficult to foresee any improvement in the predictable future. Moreover, in no year since the World War II years 1943–1945, has the rate of unemployment been as low as it was in 1953 (2.0 percent)—and in that year the nonwhite unemployment rate was 4.5 percent, or one-half of one percent above the unemployment rate for "full employment" established by the Employment Act of 1946. Thus, short of a third world war—which no sane person could possibly want—there is considerable reason to doubt the realization of sufficient tightness in the labor market to have the effect Tobin envisages.

EDUCATION

Levels and types of education are fundamental prerequisites in a society in which income and employment are based on productive efficiency—productive efficiency which, in turn, is the result of the acquisition and effective application of knowledge and skills. In the case of American blacks, where the ability to amass significant private property is limited, the acquisition of knowledge and skills provides a special sense of pride and upward mobility potential in lieu of property.

Blacks have become better educated since the end of World War II, as indicated by the following statistics:[24]

TABLE 7

Black Education

	1950	1960	1970
School Enrollment (thousands)(a)	n.a.	5910	8639
Elementary school	n.a.	4556	5993
High School	n.a.	1127	1992
College (b)	n.a.	227	654
Years of School completed by those 25 years and above (percent)(c):			
5 years or less, elem. school	32.9%	23.8%	15.1%
4 years or more high school	12.9	20.1	33.7
4 years or more of college	2.1	3.1	4.5
median years completed	6.8	8.0	9.9

(a) Blacks and other nonwhites
(b) Includes professional schools
(c) Blacks only

Despite the improvement, there are glaring disparities in black-white education. In 1972, the median number of years of school completed for persons twenty-five years and above was higher among whites than among blacks—12.2 v. 10.3; in the group 25–39 years old, however, the comparison was 12.7 v. 12.3, indicating higher educational attainment levels for blacks less than 39 years old over those beyond that age, but still showing a black-white gap. Only 5.1 percent of the black population had completed four or more years of college as compared with 12.6 percent of the white population. Almost 13 percent of the black population had less than five years of school, as compared with only 3.7 percent of whites.[25]

The causes of these disparities are many and varied. Thomas Pettigrew, the Harvard social psychologist, provided an excellent summary of these causes in 1965, which is still largely valid: "For 350 years, Negro Americans have learned that separate facilities for them almost always meant inferior facilities. Whether in the North or South, hard political realities mitigate against predominantly Negro schools receiving truly comparable instruction and facilities.... Without tracing the history of 'Negro education,' suffice it to say that the very need for the phrase—'Negro education'—signifies the long-term failure of American education to include the Negro American on fully equal terms. Even today, public education for Negroes, when compared with that for whites, remains in general 'less available, less accessible, and especially less adequate'.... Simple enumerating racial differences in years of schooling, of course, only begins to suggest the enormity of the educational hiatus between Negro and white Americans. Sadly, the blunt truth is that 'Negro education' is generally grossly inferior to 'white education' in both the North and South; it typically involves less expenditure per child, less trained and experienced teachers, and less adequate facilities; and it often prepares Negro youth through both its explicit and implicit curricula to assume only low-skilled employment befitting 'the Negro's place' as decreed by white supremacists."[26]

There can be no doubt about the disparities in the quality of education which has been made available to black and white students throughout the country. These disparities continue, so far as the predominantly nonwhite and the predominantly white schools are concerned, despite progress toward desegregation. Schools attended by white students in the past, and predominantly by these students now, generally have better qualified teachers, fewer pupils per teacher, more library volumes per student, better laboratory facilities, and more advanced courses than do all or predominantly nonwhite schools. Batchelder perceives a relationship between these black-white disparities and his third concept of intelligence, that is Intelligence C, or capabilities acquired by an individual after birth. (Intelligence A is transferred at conception, and Intelligence B is present at birth.) Batchelder observes that (1) "Southern black pupils shared discarded textbooks but had no erasers, crayons, library books, maps, or charts. Black children were confined within this system and were taught by teachers themselves miseducated in segregated schools. Black children did not acquire Intelligence C that white children acquired in public schools. Yet, when black children grow up, they must compete with better educated whites, and they must do what they can to help their children get ahead";[27] and (2) "In 1969, $59 billion, 7% of net national product, went into public and nonpublic schools (kindergarten through graduate and professional schools). Most of this schooling went to children of the nonpoor. Some went to children of the poor—but only to those in school. Of children aged 14 to 17 in 1967, 94% were in a school (83% in 1950); of children aged 18 to 19 in 1967, 48% were still in school (29% in 1950). Most of the dropouts were children of the poor who were on their way to remaining unproductive and in poverty."[28]

The incentive for blacks (and other nonwhites) to remain in school is not particularly strong when they know they are likely to (1) be employed in a job with no future, (2) experience frequent and long periods of unemployment, and (3) receive wages which are below those received by whites with fewer years of school. Increased education, although important, has not been as beneficial in terms of employment and income as might have been expected, since the movement of nonwhites into higher-paying jobs has not been commensurate with their increasing levels of education. The result has been an increasing number of nonwhites employed and working in positions that require knowledge and skills *far below* those which they possess. (It is amazing, for example, to witness the number of black B.A.s and M.A.s one encounters as skycaps at airports, bellhops in hotels, postal clerks, mail carriers, and taxi drivers.) The incommensurate returns in income are shown by the following comparisons of median incomes for black and white males in the 25-54 age group in 1969:[29]

TABLE 8

Median Incomes — Black and White

Years of School Completed		Black	White	Black income as a percentage of white income
Elementary:	Less than 8 years	$3992	$5509	71%
	8 years	4472	7018	64
High School:	1-3 years	5327	7812	68
	4 years	6192	8829	70
College:	1-3 years	7427	9831	76
	4 years or more	8669	12354	70

Thus, black men with one to three years of college had a median income which was only $409 above that of white men with an elementary schol education. The highest median income for black men (i.e, that corresponding to four or more years of college education) was less than that for white men with a high school education.

With little or no motivation or encouragement to begin with, these disparities in black-white income can be counted on to erode further the desire for an education. It is, therefore, not surprising that the high school dropout rate among 14-19-year-olds is higher for blacks than whites, as indicated by the data for 1970 in Table 9.[30]

It should also be pointed out that one of the factors causing the greater increase in the black dropout rate from fifteen to sixteen years old is the greater need in black families for additional income. Of particular significance in these data is the fact that if a black female can remain in school

TABLE 9

High School Dropouts

| | Black | | White | |
Age	Male	Female	Male	Female
Total, 14–19 years old	15.9%	13.2%	6.7%	8.1%
14 years old	0.9	2.9	1.4	1.1
15 years old	3.3	2.7	2.0	2.4
16 years old	10.9	11.1	5.0	6.7
17 years old	16.0	13.7	7.6	10.2
18 years old	29.8	27.8	13.6	14.1
19 years old	44.1	25.8	12.9	15.7

after her fourteenth year, she is less likely to drop out before reaching her nineteenth year than the black male; the white female, on the other hand, has a lower dropout rate at fourteen but after that, she is more likely to drop out than is the white male. These differences may be explained by the greater prospects for financial security in employment or marriage, or both, which the white teen-aged girl has over her black counterpart vis-à-vis their respective males, despite the tendency for white females to remain in school longer than black females.

STANDARD OF LIVING

As would be expected with rising incomes, nonwhites—as well as whites—were living longer and better in 1970 than in 1950. There are, however, significant gaps in the indicators of the longer and better life between nonwhites and whites. Following are statistics which show the improvements and gaps with respect to housing, living conditions, and health (see Table 10).[31]

Although there are no breakdowns with regard to recreational activities, nonwhites certainly accounted for a part of the following increases during the period.[32] (See Table 11.)

TABLE 10

Housing and Health

	1950 Non-white	1950 White	1960 Non-white	1960 White	1970 Non-white	1970 White
Housing:						
Owner-occupied (%)	n.a.	n.a.	38(a)%	64%	42(a)%	65%
Complete plumbing (%)	n.a.	n.a.	59(a)	88	83(a)	95
Health:						
Maternal mortality rate	2.2	0.6	1.0	0.3	0.6(b)	0.2(b)
Infant mortality rate:						
Under 28 days	27.5	19.4	26.9	17.2	23.0	14.7
28 days–11 months	16.9	7.4	16.4	5.7	11.6	4.5
Life expectancy at birth	60.8	69.1	63.6	70.6	64.6	71.7
Death rate	11.2	9.5	10.1	9.5	9.5	9.4

(a) Black only
(b) 1968

TABLE 11

Recreation

	1950	1960
Total recreational expenditures (millions of dollars)	$11,147	$39,049
Fishing licence sales (thousands)	15,338	31,136
Hunting license sales (thousands)	12,638	22,184
Attendance (thousands)		
Major league baseball	17,659	29,000
Professional basketball	1986(a)	7326
Professional football	2008	9913
Golfers (thousands)	3215	9700

(a) 1960

Yet another indication of an increasing standard of living is increased foreign travel. Again, no statistics are available on nonwhite v. white, but nonwhites—and especially blacks—assisted in effecting the following increases.[33] (See Table 12.)

TABLE 12

Foreign Travel

	1950	1960
Passports issued (thousands)(a)	300	2219
Overseas travelers (thousands)(b)	676	5260
Foreign travel expenditures (millions of dollars)	$1022	$6173
Expenditures abroad (millions of dollars)	754	3973

(a) Including an increase from 5000 to 19,000 for passports issued with Africa as the first designation.
(b) Excludes travel to Canada, Mexico, Alaska, Hawaii, Puerto Rico, and Virgin Islands, as well as cruise travelers, military personnel, and other government employees and their dependents stationed abroad, and U.S. citizens residing abroad.

Within the context of economic development, perhaps the greatest impact of a given standard of living is the effect which it has on human resources development, that is, the quality of the human resource input necessary for economic development. And, in this connection, the concept of the three types of intelligence is relevant. Assuming equality of Intelligence A between two potential births, scientific studies have shown that inequalities in Intelligence B can result from some of the consequences of low or poverty income, for example, inadequate prenatal medical care and nutrition for the prospective mother. Assuming equality of Intelligence B, disparate standards of living can produce inequalities in Intelligence C (such as postnatal care of the child, nutritional inadequacy, environmental factors in the home or neighborhood, inadequacy of educational and recreational facilities). With regard both to the transition from Intelligence A to Intelligence B and the transition from Intelligence B to Intelligence C, a low, or poverty-level income results in a disadvantaged individual. Thus, inherent in the color-caste or ethnic-caste system of the United States are standard-of-living factors which assure the perpetuation of intelligence handicaps—discrimination against nonwhites in educational, employment, and income opportunities.

SPECIAL URBAN PROBLEMS

> It is by now a relatively mundane observation to say that "race" in the literature of American race research has come to refer to "nonwhites." Indeed, the term nonwhites has, for the most part, stood for black people. In similar fashion, the expressions "urban crisis" and "urban affairs" have become polite and euphemistic ways of referring to the most important facts of urban life of the past decade; namely, the takeover of many central city areas by black people; the attendant poverty of both people and central cities; and the resultant confrontations with previously unquestioned authority.[34]

As our cities grow in size, as central or inner parts of these cities become increasingly populated by blacks and other minority groups, and as the whites continue to forsake the city for suburbia, the problems of urban life increase in variety and intensity. These problems include the deterioration of public transportation and other public services, inadequate and de facto segregated schools, insufficient parks and recreational facilities, increased ghetto and slum conditions, increased pollution, rising rates of crime and delinquency, the drug problem, health and sanitation problems, increasingly miserable housing conditions, disorganized family life, the human and economic costs of urban renewal, chaotic financial conditions, and overlapping governmental jurisdictions. A major cause of these problems is not so much that the population of the cities has increased, or that the central cities are becoming increasingly populated by blacks and other minorities, as it is the fact that there are not sufficient jobs for those who migrate to the cities in the hope of escaping from the miseries and perils of rural life and, in some instances, life in the South.

The extent to which it is possible to identify urban problems with the problems of black people is suggested by only too familiar statistics. For example, in 1970, not only did 74 percent of the total black population live in metropolitan areas (with 58 percent living in the inner city), but (1) inner-city blacks as a percentage of total inner-city populations ranged between 11 percent (cities with less than 250,000 people) and 28 percent (cities with populations of 2 million); (2) *blacks accounted for between 18 percent and 71 percent of the populations of the country's ten largest cities;* (3) almost half (48 percent) of the total black population was concentrated in thirty cities, with more than one-third living in fifteen cities; and (4) in those thirty urban areas with the highest proportion of blacks, the percentages ranged from 43.6 percent to 82.3 percent.[35] Thus, urban problems are, to a very considerable extent, the problems of black people—and many (if not most) of these problems are associated with relatively low levels of economic development in these urban areas.

BLACK BUSINESS ENTERPRISE

According to the U.S. Bureau of the Census, in 1969—the latest year for which official statistics are available—there were 163,000 black-owned firms, and these firms had business receipts of $4.5 billion. The number of black-owned enterprises amounted to 2.2 percent of all firms then in the country (50.6 percent of all minority-owned firms) and the business receipts were 0.3 percent of the total receipts of all enterprises (42.4 percent of the receipts of all minority-owned firms).

The black-owned enterprises and their business receipts, in 1969, were distributed as follows:[36]

TABLE 13

Black-Owned Businesses

Category	Number of Firms (in thousands)		Business Receipts (billions of dollars)	
	Amount	Percentage	Amount	Percentage
Selected services	56	34.4%	$0.7	15.6%
Retail trade	45	27.6	1.9	42.2
Transportation and public utilities	17	10.4	0.2	4.4
Contract construction	16	9.8	0.5	11.1
Finance, insurance, real estate	8	4.9	0.3	6.7
Manufacturers	3	1.8	0.3	6.7
Wholesale trade	1	0.7	0.4	8.9
Other	17	10.4	0.2	4.4
	163	100.0%	$4.5	100.0%

Although the number of firms and business receipts may have increased since 1969, a safe assumption is that there have been no significant shifts in the relative distribution of either.

SUMMARY

In terms of income, nonwhites gained absolutely but not in relation to gains made by whites during the 1950–1970 period. For example, between 1947 and 1969, median income increased by approximately 130 percent for nonwhites and 90 percent for whites. The number of nonwhite families with an income of $10,000 or more increased by about 700 percent as compared with approximately 300 percent for whites. The number of families receiving $3000 or less decreased about the same for both groups, 65 percent. The number of nonwhites in poverty decreased from 56 percent to 32 percent during the 1960s, but the nonwhite percentage *was still more than three times* the white percentage. It should be emphasized that at any given level of income (1) more members of nonwhite families had to be engaged in earning that income than was true of white families, and (2) a higher level of education was required of nonwhites than whites.

Comparisons of employment by occupation show that nonwhites made more significant progress, in percentage terms, than did whites in moving into the better-paying occupations. For example, between 1960 and 1970, the average *increase* of nonwhites in professional, technical, managerial, official, proprietor, clerical, sales, craftsmen, foremen, and operative positions was 84 percent. The average increase for whites was 23.2 percent. With regard to the lower-paying positions or private household workers, farmers and farm workers, the average decrease was 47.5 percent for nonwhites and 22 percent for whites. Despite this progress, the underrepresentation of nonwhites in the better-paying positions was not appreciably altered (i.e., an average of 5.2 percent in 1960 v. 7.3 percent in 1970), and the nonwhite share in the lower-paid positions was still proportionately large in 1970 (i.e., 26.5 percent).

In education, blacks reduced their overall illiteracy rate by 52 percent between 1959 and 1969; it was 56 percent for whites. The percentage of the population 25–29 years old who had completed four years or more of high school, between 1960 and 1970, increased 17.5 points for blacks (to 56 percent) and by 13.5 percent for whites (to 77.5 percent). The percentage increase in the population 25–34 years old who had completed four years of college between 1960 and 1970 was roughly the same (i.e., 30 percent). The median years of school completed in 1970 for blacks and whites differed to an increasingly significant degree when progressively older age groups are compared—12.4 for black v. 12.8 for whites in the 20–21 age group, 4.6 for blacks v. 8.6 for whites in the age group of 75 years and above, and averages for all age groups of 9.8 for blacks and 12.7 for whites. Thus, to the degree that educational attainment is a determinant of employment and income, blacks were still more disadvantaged than whites. It has already been noted, however, that given levels of education result in disparate employment and income opportunities for blacks and whites.

Between 1960 and 1970, the rate of owner-occupied housing among blacks increased from 38 percent to 42 percent, as compared to the slight increase from 64 percent to 65 percent for whites; thus, the ratio of black owner-occupancy to white owner-occupancy increased from 59.4 to 64.6. The greatest increase in the home-ownership rate for blacks, however, occurred in nonmetropolitan areas (i.e., from 35 percent to 39 percent for metropolitan areas, and from 31 percent to 35 percent for central cities). An increase in suburban homeownership for blacks also occurred, from 52 percent to 54 percent. With respect to urban living, it is significant that while the black renter-occupied rate in nonmetropolitan areas decreased from 0.9 percent to 0.7 percent, the rate in metropolitan areas increased from 2.3 percent to 2.9 percent, and in central cities from 2.0 percent to 2.5 percent. The significance lies in the larger number of blacks in 1970 than in 1960 who were subjected to the merciless and unscrupulous behavior of urban slum landlords—as well as to the unethical (if not criminal) business practices of ghetto merchants in these neighborhoods. Regarding other aspects and reflections of the standard of living, improvements in life expectancy, maternal and infant mortality rates, and in general health for blacks and other nonwhites have been noted. There were, however, the usual gaps when these data were compared with white data.

Black business enterprises account for just over two percent of the total businesses in the country, and for less than one-half of one percent of total business receipts. Almost three-fourths of these enterprises are to be found in selected services (including barber shops, beauty parlors, and funeral homes), retail trade, and transportation and public utilities (mainly taxi-cabs) categories.

Chapter Three

Obstacles to Black Economic Development

Economic development results from the interactions of human resources with the other factors of production. Much of the literature on economic development, at least until fairly recently, tended to ignore—or took for granted—the role of human behavior in the economic development process. Sir W. Arthur Lewis, internationally known West Indian development economist, must be given credit for much of the pioneering research on the relationship between human behavior and economic development. Having established these relationships, Lewis noted, "... it is necessary to enquire into the differences in human behavior which influence economic growth. The enquiry into the human actions has to be conducted at different levels, because they are proximate causes of growth, as well as causes of these causes. The proximate causes are principally three. First, there is the [will] to economize [illustrated by the desire for goods and the cost of effort to obtain them].... If the effort is not made, either because the desire to economize does not exist, or else because either custom or institutions discourage its expression, then economic growth will not occur. Secondly, there is the increase of knowledge and its application. This process has occurred throughout human history, but the more rapid growth of output in recent centuries is associated obviously with the more rapid accumulation and application of knowledge in production. And thirdly, growth depends upon increasing the amount of capital or other resources per head."[1] The rationale of human actions as they relate to black economic development is the concern of this chapter.[2]

RESISTANCE TO CHANGE

We are living in a world of constant and accelerating changes. There is considerable justification for the contention that more change has occurred in the past fifty years than took place in the 2000 or more years before. Kurt W. Marek, who wrote *Gods, Graves and Scholars* under the name of C. W. Ceram, notes that, "We, in the twentieth century, are concluding an era of mankind five thousand years in length."[3] Kenneth Boulding, the economist, has observed that, "As far as many statistical series related to activities of mankind are concerned, the date that divides human history into two equal parts is well within living memory. . . . The world of today . . . is as different from the world in which I was born as that world was from Julius Caesar's. . . . Almost as much has happened since I was born as happened before."[4] If the last 50,000 years of man's existence were divided into lifetimes of sixty-two years each, there would be 800 such lifetimes, and Alvin Toffler has said that, "Of these 800, fully 650 were spent in caves. Only during the last seventy lifetimes has it been possible to communicate effectively from one lifetime to another—as writing made it possible to do. Only during the last six lifetimes did masses of men ever see a printed word. Only during the last four has it been possible to measure time with any precision. Only in the last two has anyone anywhere used an electric motor. And the overwhelming majority of all the material goods we use in daily life today have been developed within the present, the 800th lifetime. This 800th lifetime marks a sharp break with all past human experience because during this lifetime man's relationship to resources has reversed itself. This is the most evident in the field of economic development. Within a single lifetime, agriculture, the original basis of civilization, has lost its dominance in nation after nation."[5] In the memories of many of us, there was no radio or television, ground speeds of a mile a minute and air travel were unheard of, there were no computers, synthetic fibers were unknown, and many of the other things which are now regarded as necessities were only dreams, if that.

It is not only the changes in material things that have occurred, however: "Change . . . spawns in its wake all sorts of curious social flora—from psychedelic churches and 'free universities' to science cities in the Arctic and wife-swapping clubs in California. It breeds odd personalities, too: children who at twelve are no longer childlike; adults who at fifty are children of twelve. There are rich men who play–act poverty, computer programmers who turn on with LSD. There are anarchists who, beneath their dirty denim shirts, are outrageous conformists, and conformists who, beneath their button-down collars, are outrageous anarchists. There are married priests and atheist ministers and Jewish Zen Buddhists. We have pop . . . and op . . . and *art cinétique*. . . . There are Playboy Clubs and homosexual movie theaters . . . amphetamines and tranquilizers . . . anger, affluence, and oblivion. Much oblivion."[6] Toffler continues and observes: "Change is the process by which the future invades our lives, and it is important to look at it closely, not merely from the ground perspectives of history, but also from the vantage point of the living, breathing individuals who experience it. The acceleration of change in our time is, itself, an elemental force. This accelerative thrust has personal and psychological, as well as sociological consequences."[7]

Despite this evidence of change, the tendency to look back is strong in the black community—the venerable Satchel Paige's sage advice, not to look backward for fear someone may be gaining on you, notwithstanding. What was good enough for past generations does not suffice for the current one, and what is good enough for the current generation may be even less sufficient for future generations. In some very fundamental ways—perhaps in ways that hurt—there must be a break with the past if black economic development is to go forward. One area in which such a break is most needed is black education. For example, too many predominantly black colleges are still adhering to a liberal-arts type of curriculum, instituted when the colleges were founded—and several of these colleges are more than a century old. Their refusal to react positively to technological and other changes in the real world results in the graduation of young people who are not ideally suited either for the world of work or for graduate studies leading to promising careers in that world.

Another area of extreme significance to black folk—at least in the recent past so that the effects are still evident—is religion. Sir Arthur Lewis, referred to earlier, has examined the relationships between religion and economic development.[8] Some of his conclusions are applicable to the current state of black economic development. He finds, for example, that the process of economic development is adversely impacted, if not severely frustrated, when religion (1) discourages the desire for material things; (2) emphasizes the devotion of the mind to spiritual contemplation as opposed to concern about the most efficient combination and utilization of economic resources; (3) stresses man as merely one manifestation of God rather than as the center of the universe for whom all else exists for his gratification and convenience; and/or (4) favors the status quo in socioeconomic relationships and emphasizes the virtues of obedience, duty, and obligation above socioeconomic benefits which might result from changing the status quo.

Lewis is also quick to point out that not all religions, as a result of these and other characteristics, are antagonistic to economic development—and that, in the case of minorities, religion often has salutary effects in that it is the one force which often binds these minorities together. Nonetheless, sufficient evidence exists of incompatibilities between religion and economic development. The "you-take-the-world-and-give-me-Jesus" philosophy, tithing with the only visible effect being an ostentatious building and/or a well-kept pastor, and the observed conflicts between the tenets of religion and the realities of life all underscore the point being made.

A postscript should be added which recognizes an increasing sense of socioeconomic responsibility on the part of an increasing number of clergymen and churches in the black community, such as Freedom Enterprises in Philadelphia, Operation Breadbasket, Operation PUSH in Chicago, and others. So far as the less conventional religions are concerned, cognizance must also be taken of the strong economic underpinning and philosophies of such religious organizations as the late Father Divine's in Philadelphia and elsewhere and that of the Black Muslims. Would that there were more examples than there are. What appears to be necessary, to use the terminology of H. Richard Niebahr, is a greater adherence to the "I–You" concept of religion as a complement to the "I–Thou" concept on which most black religions appear to be based. The "I–You" concept, basically, means a responsibility to society and presupposes not necessarily an effacing of self but the recognition of self as a responsible part of the larger society.[9]

IMAGE OF SELF

Until fairly recently, the black man's image of himself was stigmatized solely because he was black. His consequent rejection of himself was moot testimony to the effectiveness of white America's persistent and penetrating insistence on white supremacy and superiority. White was associated with rightness and goodness; black was associated with wrongness and badness. White was beautiful; black was ugly. The result of this low esteem of oneself, of course, breeds a lack of belief in oneself. Not believing in basic self-worth, in turn, had adverse consequences for black ambition and motivation. Being constantly told that he was inferior, and not being able to contradict these changes—because the educational system went to great pains (and still does) to ensure an unawareness that blacks had ever made a contribution beyond menial and back-breaking work—the tendency of many blacks was to conform—or, at least, appear to conform—to the degrading stereotype systematically created and kept alive by the doctrine of white supremacy.

The stereotype is, of course, at great variance with the black man's past. Melville Herskovits in *The Myth of the Negro Past* emphasized the extent to which the African background has been either ignored or misinterpreted in most of the research studies conducted on American blacks.[10] Critical historians and other social scientists have established that the black American's past goes back at least to the late Stone Age—prior to 5000 B.C.—when, according to *Hammond's Graphic History of Mankind*, blacks arrived in Africa from Asia. In the period of time between then and 1619, when Africans were first brought to the United States as indentured servants, a glorious black history had been established. Even if the Assyrian and Babylonian empires and the Hittite and Egyptian kingdoms are excluded, as some are wont to do on the dubious grounds that these were not black people, there would still be the powerful and undeniably black kingdoms of Ghana, Mali, Bornu, Baguirmi, Songhay and Benin between 700 A.D. and the beginning of the slave trade in the earliest years of the seventeenth century. Prior to their becoming merchandise themselves, the merchants of these great kingdoms in West Africa conducted a prosperous trade throughout North Africa as well as in parts of Europe and Asia. Art, in practically all its forms, was highly developed—Benin bronze, Nok clay, and Ife stone are still highly valued by art collectors. Even as late as the sixteenth century, viable and prosperous business activities, based largely on specialized skills such as weaving, pottery-making, woodworking, and metallurgy, continued, despite the decline of these kingdoms and the subsequent resurgence of tribalism.

Elements of this past survived after blacks were forcibly brought to the New World and subjected to the most inhumane system of slavery in recorded history. During slavery, during the lowest point in American race relations (i.e., the post-Reconstruction period of 1877–1901) and since, these ties to a once-glorious past not only survived but were nurtured. This is somewhat surprising, in that there was little, or nothing, that the black man could learn of his own past from the public educational systems except that which was sordid or degrading. Nevertheless, it was increasing knowledge of this past, coupled with the increasing number of newly politically independent nations in black Africa, that accelerated the struggle for identity, dignity, recognition, and status that characterized the Black Revolution of the post-World War II period.

That whites were determined to sever the black man from his past, however, is evidenced by a most deliberate, systematic, and persistent brainwashing. The constitutionalized concept of blacks as something less than human and, therefore, not entitled to basic human rights, developed during slavery, did not disappear with the Emancipation Proclamation or the passage of the Fourteenth Amendment to the Constitution.[11] Beginning with the post-Reconstruction period, the inferior status of blacks and the privileged and superior status of whites were articulated—and enforced, when necessary, by political power.[12] Supported by an educational system that completely denied any worthwhile contributions by blacks to the historical development of man, the brainwashing forced blacks to view themselves through the eyes of white America. Thus, for the majority of black Americans, their image of self became what white America's negative reinforcement intended it to be—i.e., an inferior being who saw in his blackness everything of which to be ashamed and nothing of which to be proud.

The success attending this brainwashing is suggested by the following. In 1939, a noted black psychologist, Kenneth B. Clark, conducted an experiment in which he asked a group of black children in the North to select a "nice doll," having a choice between white and brown dolls. The white doll was selected by 68 percent of these children. Twenty-eight years later, Stephen Asher and Vernon Allen conducted a similar experiment in Newark, N. J. This time, 186 black and 155 white children were used in the experiment. The somewhat surprising result of this experiment was that *76 percent* of each group of children picked the white doll as the "nice" one.[13] The results of the latter experiment are somewhat surprising because 1967 was the year of the violent unrest and rebellion by blacks in Detroit, Grand Rapids, Houston, Newark, Oakland, and other urban areas across the country—preceded, it will be recalled, by similar rebellions in the earlier years of the 1960s in Chicago, New York, Rochester, and the Watts area of Los Angeles. In 1967, also, the slogan "Black Power" had been adopted, and the book written by Charles Hamilton and Stokely Carmichael entitled *Black Power* was published. Thus, despite the fact that black people had experienced some successes in the struggle for identity and dignity by 1967, the racial superiority–inferiority nonsense—conceived originally to rationalize and justify the most despicably dehumanizing system of slavery in recorded history, and perpetuated after slavery in support, among other things, of capitalism and the profit motive—was still deeply ingrained in the psyche of black people.

Vestiges of this inferior and degrading self-image still

exist in the black community. Until it is completely supplanted by a pervading pride in self, black economic development will continue to be hampered.

POWERLESSNESS

Closely associated with the black's image of self—in that it represents a swing of the pendulum too far in the opposite direction—is the illusion of power. As country after country in Africa achieved political independence, awareness of self, identity, and pride in self grew in the black community. This increased awareness, identity, and pride coincided with (or resulted in) some civil rights victories—and blacks began to believe their own slogans and rhetoric. So, logically, if you have power, why bother about economic development? The basic premise is ridiculous!

Blacks in the United States are a relatively powerless people. Less than one-half of one percent of all business assets in the country are owned by blacks. Despite progress made in elections from 1962 until the present, blacks are still underrepresented in national and state legislative bodies. Only about 2 percent of all black members of the Armed Services are officers (as compared with about 13 percent of whites). Blacks are grossly underrepresented in the news media, country-wide. Less than 3 percent of all blacks employed in all types of organizations throughout the country are in decision-making positions.

According to the estimate one selects, black Americans spend annually between $30 and $60 billion. The ego of black Americans tends to become inflated when it is realized that they spend more per year for goods and services than is produced by every other country in the world except Canada, France, Germany, Italy, Japan, and the United Kingdom. Assuming only the estimate of $30 billion, and assuming a United States black population of 23 million, the per capita black expenditures exceed the per capita gross national product of all but seventeen countries or territories in the world (Australia, Austria, Belgium, Canada, Denmark, Finland, France, Germany, Italy, Japan, Luxemburg, New Zealand, Norway, Puerto Rico, Sweden, Switzerland, and the United Kingdom). The meaningful comparisons, however, should be within the context of the economy of this country—and when these comparisons are made, the relative powerlessness of black Americans is underscored. Even assuming a $40 billion level of expenditures, in 1971 this was less than the reported assets of General Motors, Standard Oil of New Jersey, and International Telephone and Telegraph; less than the reported sales of General Motors and Standard Oil of New Jersey; less than stockholders' equities in Standard Oil of New Jersey, General Motors, Texaco, IBM, Ford Motor Company, and Gulf Oil; about 5 percent of the assets of nonbanking financial institutions in this country; and less than 4 percent of the gross national product. Again, assuming the $40-billion level, if this had been distributed evenly between all black families in 1968, it would have resulted in an average income per family of *$438 less* than the median white income in that year.

The real seat of power in our society is economic—and difficult as were the political and social victories won by the various types of civil rights actions, that difficulty is child's play compared to getting the white man in this country to share that economic power with blacks, or any other minority. He is even unwilling to share that power with his own women, as the rampant sexual discrimination in employment opportunities bears witness to. Blacks are given impressive titles with handsome salaries, expense accounts, secretaries, plush offices, and, in some cases, even automobiles at their disposal; they are seldom, if ever, admitted to the inner sanctum where policy is determined and decisions are made, however.

ALIENATION

A Louis Harris poll in November, 1972, found that 69 percent of blacks felt largely alienated from the system in which they lived. The mood of alienation was reflected in how blacks responded to questions about whether they felt that (1) tax laws were written to help the rich but not the average man; (2) the rich get richer and the poor get poorer; (3) what they thought did not count for much; (4) people running the country do not care what happens to them; (5) people with power were out to take advantage of them; and (6) they were left out of things around them. Interestingly, on all these indicators, the sense of alienation in 1972 was greater or more intense than in 1966. Blacks (and other minorities) are aware, for example, that the big housing subsidies benefit the middle classes and the wealthy, through federal tax deductions of local real estate and property taxes, and that indirect housing subsidies to the middle class and the wealthy amount to about $6 billion a year as compared with $2 billion a year for directly subsidized housing for the poor. The powerlessness and voicelessness, from which this sense of alienation springs, are manifested by little or no participation in decisions which have profoundly adverse economic and social consequences for minorities. These decisions encompass such important matters as highway development, health and welfare programs, educational programs, urban renewal, community development, poverty programs, and revenue-sharing.

An increasing number of blacks, in recent years, have come to the conclusion that the only manner by which racial equality can become a reality is by blacks (1) gaining complete control of the institutions of power, and (2) ousting "establishment" businessmen, professionals, and officials from black communities. This belief, which is clothed in the ideological garb of Black Separatism, is considered by its adherents as the most effective means of replacing self-hatred and disdain with black pride and self-respect, and of dealing with the alienating nature of the establishment. (With the Mexican-Americans or Chicanos, much the same sentiment is embodied in the concept of *La Raza* and in the rallying cry, *La Causa.*)

It is because of alienation that some economists are beginning to raise serious questions about the traditional concepts of economics as a discipline. For example, according to some, the preoccupation with gross national product puts emphasis on economic growth as a measure of economic benefits. To the extent that this is true, so goes the thesis, economics becomes value-empty, which contributes to alienation by neglecting nonmaterial, intellectual, psychological, and spiritual human needs. To the extent that this is a correct analysis, the questions raised include the relevance and applicability of some of the fundamental assumptions of contemporary theoretical and practical economics to current socioeconomic problems, including black economic development. The relevance and application of current theoretical and practical economics to black economic development is explored in the final chapter of this book.

COMPENSATORY CONSUMPTION

During the early part of this century, Thorstein Veblen, a penetrating critic of socioeconomic institutions of America, pointed out in *The Theory of the Leisure Class* that much of the consumption of the well-to-do class was of doubtful value, and that it was motivated by a desire to impress others by a demonstration of superior power and prestige, by their ability to live extravagantly. Veblen termed this "conspicuous consumption." Black Americans also demonstrate some of these characteristics, but—at least in the opinion of this writer—this type of consumption is motivated as much, if not more, by compensatory as by conspicuous considerations. For people who historically have been deprived of much of this world's material goods, the acquisition of such items as television sets, automobiles, and sundry household appliances becomes a major achievement.

The consequences of compensatory consumption for black economic development is at least twofold. First, it usually means a flow of money *out* of the black community. In many instances, the volume of this outflow is enormously enlarged by the exploitative prices charged for the articles and by usurious installment and interest charges. Only a small percentage of this money is returned to the black community in the form of jobs and wages or other types of income to black people.

A second consequence of compensatory consumption is the attitude it engenders in whites toward blacks. Many whites are of the opinion that blacks are not deserving of any type of assistance because, in addition to a perceived black aversion to work, there is at least one automobile parked in front, and a TV aerial on the roof, of every home occupied by blacks, regardless of how dilapidated the house may be. The speciousness of this attitude should be obvious. First, blacks need automobiles for transportation to and from work and to obtain essential services, either because employment opportunity and sources of services are far removed, or public transportation does not serve the areas in which blacks are forced to live. Second, of the 15.1 percent of blacks with four years or less of elementary school completed in 1970,[14] there was a significant number of illiterates;[15] the possession of a television set kept them from being totally ignorant about events in the society and the world in which they live. Third, the attitude is inconsistent with the facts about ownership of luxury items by blacks. For example, in 1970, only 37.3 percent of blacks owned an automobile, while 51.9 percent of whites did; 13.4 percent of the black population owned two or more automobiles, as compared with 31.0 percent of whites; 10.7 percent of blacks owned one or more recent-make automobiles as compared with 22.4 percent of whites;

83.4 percent of blacks owned black-and-white TV sets, as compared with 76.8 percent of whites—but black-and-white TV sets are no longer a "status symbol," so 17.4 percent of blacks owned color TV as compared with 40.1 percent of whites; and 3.9 percent of blacks owned dishwashers, as compared with 18.8 percent of whites.[16]

POVERTY AND RELATED CONDITIONS

The criteria used to define poverty are painfully applicable to America's black population. Improvements in the socioeconomic status of blacks during this century, and especially during the past two decades, indicate how far blacks were below the average for the country in terms of all standards of socioeconomic well-being. And, the existing gaps between blacks and whites with respect to these same standards underscore that which remains to be accomplished in terms of productive, consumptive, and other inequalities between blacks and whites.

Poverty has been defined by Lester C. Thurow in *Poverty and Discrimination* with reference to four varied bases.[17] These are (1) "A fraction of the income distribution," (2) "Explicit goals for the relative shape of income distribution," (3) "Estimates of the minimum income level necessary to guarantee healthy survival," and (4) "Adequate standards of living as seen by the majority of the population." Black poverty, with respect to the first basis, was discussed in the preceding chapter.[18] The second definition of poverty classifies as poor anyone who falls below 50 percent of the median income. In 1971, approximately 40 percent of nonwhite families and about 16 percent of white families were poor according to this criterion.[19] The third definition takes into account "the estimated costs of minimum amounts of shelter, clothing and food." If an income of $3000 can be considered as adequate for these purposes, which is extremely doubtful, 19.4 percent of nonwhite families and 6.9 percent of white families in 1971 qualified under this definition of poverty.[20] With respect to the fourth definition, an official poverty level was defined by the 1971 Current Population Survey, the core of which is the nutritionally-adequate food plan designed by the U.S. Department of Agriculture. The low-income threshold for a nonfarm family of four, according to this survey, was $3968 in 1970. Almost one-third of the black families but only about one-eighth of the white families were in poverty according to this definition. Or, if the index centering around the Department of Agriculture's Economy Food Plan is used as a criterion, 30.9 percent of nonwhite families but only 9.9 percent of white families were in poverty in 1971.[21] Thus, by either of these definitions, somewhere between roughly one-fifth and two-fifths of all nonwhite families in the United States were poor in 1971, as compared to between approximately one-twelfth and one-fifth of white families.

The psychological costs of black poverty are, in a word, horrendous. Living in vermin-infested urban ghettos or chronically depressed rural areas, deprived of the minimum necessities for a socially acceptable existence, watching helplessly while loved ones slowly die of hunger or disease, provided with inferior education (if any at all), lacking adequate facilities for wholesome recreation and social life, constantly victimized by unscrupulous merchants and landlords—these are conditions which not only sap physical and mental vigor, but are psychologically damaging. The fact that these conditions persist in a society which constantly reminds itself—with justification—that it is the most affluent the world has ever known adds greatly to the problem. And, very unfortunately, the effects of poverty are not limited to those experiencing the trauma—their progeny are also affected, and for generations to come.

A factor often related to black poverty, especially by those who are most critical, is the presumed lack of motivation among blacks—it is often claimed that the lack of motivation is a major cause of the lowly socioeconomic status of black people. Motivation by definition cannot be an innate characteristic. It is an attribute influenced by one's environment. For generations, black motivation has been crushed or adversely influenced by inequalities which are, in turn, related to deprivation, subjugation, and rejection. For example, blacks are aware that (1) black males who bring to the labor market a background of four or more years of college education can hope for an income of only about 70 percent of what white males with a similar level of educational attainment can expect, and only about 98 percent of what a white male with only a high school education can expect to earn; (2) black males with a high school education can expect to earn about 89 percent of what white males with only an elementary school education can earn; (3) median black family income is only about 60 percent of that of white families, regardless of education; (4) it takes more than two wage-earners in a black family to earn as much as one wage-earner in a white family, on the average; (5) the percentage of black families in poverty is more than three times that of white poor families, even among those who are fully employed; (6) the unemployment rate among blacks has been consistently twice as high as that of whites since 1954; and (7) regardless of levels of educational attainment, the concentration of black members in the labor force is greater in the lower-paying jobs.[22] Under this set of circumstances, motivation can be—and often is—effectively frustrated. The end result of these and other black-white disparities has been the development and perpetuation of a sense of powerlessness, hopelessness, and defeatism.

Another poverty-related factor, with strong sociopsychological implications, is the extremely important role of the black female. The strong matriarchal nature of the slave family has persisted in the postslavery culture of black people—but for different reasons. In the latter part of the nineteenth century and the early part of the twentieth, social disorganization of black life in the United States resulted in the continuation of the "mother-centered family with its emphasis on the primacy of the mother-child relation and only tenuous ties to a man."[23] With the gradual movement of the black population from rural areas in the South to urban areas in the North and West, it was always easier for the black female to find employment than it was for the black male. Moreover, thanks to the misguided administration of our welfare system, it was (and is) much easier for a family to qualify for public assistance if there were (and is) no man in residence. Thus, faced with inabilities to obtain employment in their new urban environment, and knowing that their families are unlikely to receive necessary public assistance if they remain at home, large numbers of black husbands and fathers have deserted. It should be emphasized here that separations among black rural couples compared to those among white rural couples are less frequent. This is a primary cause of (1) the great disparity in the percentages of female heads of households between blacks and whites (in 1971, the percentage for black families was about three times that for white families); and (2) the larger percentage of black female-headed families living in poverty (with an income of less than $3000) than for white heads of household (in 1969, 58 v. 29 percent).[24]

There is, of course, a relationship between the highly matriarchal nature of the black culture and certain socially undesirable attitudinal and behavioral patterns within that culture. Many, and available studies and research suggest that most, of these patterns result less from any inherent traits of blacks and more from the special set of conditions under which they are born and must live. The importance of employment and income, as aspects of these conditions, was mentioned earlier. Not brought out were the pressures upon blacks to live in well-defined areas, geographically separated from whites, regardless of socioeconomic status. A detailed examination of life under racially–segregated residential patterns leads one to the inevitable conclusion that conditions of life in the black community are more likely to produce antisocial than socially accepted attitudes and behavior. The geographical restrictions imposed upon blacks in terms of where they can live result in a higher concentration of blacks both in neighborhoods and in dwellings. The public services provided to these all-black communities—i.e., transportation, garbage and trash collection, recreational facilities, etc. —are notoriously and universally inadequate. Also, since only 38 percent of the black housing in metropolitan areas is owner-occupied—as compared with 62 percent of white housing in these areas[25]—black-housing maintenance often leaves a great deal to be desired, either because of a lack of interest on the part of the absentee landlord, financial inability, or lack of incentive on the part of the tenants, or both. Thus, blacks are forced to coexist with rats and other vermin, both in the streets and in the houses in which they live—with the streets usually being the more attractive of two undesirables. Further, in view of the large percentage of female-headed families among blacks, and the relatively low level of income received by these women, their children are often left to their own devices for considerable portions of the day because either the women cannot afford to pay for child-care services or day-care centers are either nonexistent or inadequate.

INSTITUTIONALIZED RACIAL DISCRIMINATION

Black poverty, compensatory consumption, alienation, and self-image are intimately related to the impact of the all-pervading racial discrimination in our society. This relationship was touched on in the discussion of each of these four subjects. It is of sufficient importance in and of itself, as an obstacle to black economic development, to warrant special attention as a psychological impediment to black economic and other progress.

Racial discrimination, as used herein, means all overt

not, is that the adaptation to racial discrimination produces objective differences which tend to justify differential treatment.

The preconceived stereotypical characterization of blacks—one manifestation of racially discriminatory behavior—has given rise to some invidious generalizations. One of these, which has gained increasing popularity in recent years, is that blacks have little desire to work—and, if they happen also to be poor, the work ethic is missing altogether. Those who subscribe to this view appear to be completely oblivious to the growing number of studies which invalidate the generalization. For example, Leonard Goodwin in *Do the Poor Want Work?* has found that the poor—including blacks and whites, males and females, youths and adults, as well as those receiving welfare—"have a strong work ethic and do not need to be taught the importance of work—that they identify their self-esteem with work as strongly as do the nonpoor.... The ways in which the poor differ from the affluent can reasonably be attributed to their different experiences of success and failure in the world."[31] Edward Simpkins, special assistant to the vice-president for urban affairs at Wayne State University, observed that, "In the 20th century urban metropolis, one finds willing workers but no jobs more frequently than one finds nonwilling workers amid an abundance of jobs. And in rural areas one finds privation among some who believe very strongly in the work ethic and who do work, but who fail to manage to provide more than a subsistence income for their families."[32] Statistics on the working poor tend to substantiate the findings and views of Goodwin and Simpkins.[33] The 300-year work record of blacks in the United States should leave no doubt about their performance in hard and honest work. Belief in the work ethic, however, is eroded if formidable obstacles to finding employment persist, and if there is continued denial of just rewards for work. The special obstacles to finding employ-

about their position in the system, but, when they do become concerned, victimization takes on important social psychological dimensions. Individuals then suffer feelings of 'relative deprivation' which give rise to reactions ranging from despair, apathy, and withdrawal to covert and overt aggressions."[29]

The social-psychological dimensions of victimization caused by racial discrimination are varied. For example, one important consequence is that blacks may be hesitant to make investments in themselves, in their own intellectual and professional development, than might be the case in the absence of such discrimination. In 1969, for example, the median income of white men with less than eight years of elementary education was $180 more than that of black men with 1–3 years of high school education, and the median income for white men with four years of high school education was $160 more than that of black men with four or more years of college education. Using 1970 data, the median income for black men increased to only $4677 from $3922 for less than eight years of elementary education and to $8669 for four years or more of college education; on the other hand, the median income for white men increased by $6845, from $5509 to $12,354.[30] Thus, the financial incentive for blacks to invest in education is much less than it is for whites. This decreased incentive to invest in one's own intellectual and professional development is at least partially responsible for the higher school dropout rate and the lower college enrollment of blacks.

Another result of racial discrimination, which is psychological but which has important economic consequences, is its self-fulfilling nature. When subjected to racial discrimination—accompanied by systematic and consistent humiliation and rejection—over a period of time, there is a tendency for those discriminated against to adjust their behavior and expectations to fit the stereotypes imposed upon them by the majority members of society. The result, more often than

and in the receipt of certain essential public services—health, sanitation, recreation. Discrimination through monopoly power is the exclusion of black factors of production from those areas where monopolies result in factor returns above those prevailing in a competitive economy. In pricing, racial discrimination is manifested by blacks having to pay above-market prices for what is bought while receiving below-market prices for what is sold. That blacks receive less than whites for the major commodity they have to sell—their labor power—was documented earlier. That they have to pay more than whites for comparable housing, food and the other necessities of life has been amply documented by several studies.[28]

Racial discrimination is manifested in yet other ways. For example, blacks are (1) taxed on the same basis as whites but are not accorded the same representation in government or provided the same services for which they pay taxes; (2) forced to fight wars in foreign lands to secure rights for others, which are denied to them in their own country; (3) deprived of their land and homes—often under the guise of eminent domain, the right of government to appropriate private property for public use—in order to further the interests of majority whites (highway development and urban renewal); and (4) guaranteed certain rights by the Constitution but are imprisoned, beaten, and sometimes killed if and when they attempt to exercise these rights. In short, barriers are created and excuses devised to prevent blacks from enjoying a modicum of the freedom, rights, and privileges which are considered as legitimate in every way for white Americans.

Racial discrimination, thus, means so many kinds of victimization of blacks. St. Clair Drake has taken note of the types of victimization and their consequences. He observes, for example, that "Individual 'victims' may or may not accept the rationalization given for the denial to them of power and prestige. They may or may not be aware of and concerned

and covert psychologically relevant attitudes, perceptions, values, criteria, and institutions of the majority society which result in differential and objectively irrational decisions and actions with respect to and affecting the black minority. Further, there is substantial evidence—in the history of the United States (and of the Union of South Africa) as opposed to the histories of, say, Egypt, Greece, Brazil, Hawaii, and New Zealand—of the thesis that racial discrimination is more a function of certain types of socioeconomic systems than of biological differences or of other factors. It is a firmly entrenched characteristic of our society that is used to subordinate and repress blacks (and other nonwhites) living in that society. It is an institutionalized and integral part of the economic, political, and social systems which operate—overtly or covertly—to ensure that blacks (and other nonwhites) will remain in a disadvantaged and inferior state. In the words used by the National Advisory Commission on Civil Disorders (the Kerner Commission), "The prejudice against color in America has formed a bar to advancement unlike any other."[26]

The forms which this discrimination takes are varied.[27] In employment, it results in larger than proportionate unemployment, the concentration of blacks in the lower-paying jobs, part-time employment, and (eventually) in the "discouraged worker" (i.e., an unemployed person who has given up looking for work and who becomes a voluntary nonparticipant in the labor force). In wages, it means that blacks are paid less than whites for the same work. Racial discrimination in occupation results in a concentration of blacks in the low-income jobs and the reservation of higher-income jobs for whites; if the better-paying jobs are not explicitly reserved for whites, the job specifications are drawn up in ways that past discrimination in education and employment opportunities disqualify blacks. The consequences of racial discrimination in human investment are most evident in disparities in expenditures for educating blacks and whites,

ment by blacks are evidenced by the racial differentials in unemployment rates, discussed earlier.

SUMMARY

Black economic development is impeded by most of the factors generally associated with undevelopment or underdevelopment—low incomes; disproportionately large concentrations in unskilled or, at best, semi-skilled jobs; relatively lower levels of educational and skill attainments; underutilization of manpower; relatively low marginal productivity of labor; inadequate capital accumulation; and so forth. In addition to these obstacles, and perhaps more important, are phenomena which tend to freeze blacks in their low socioeconomic status or which tend to reinforce that status. These phenomena, which are mainly sociopsychological in nature, include resistance to change, an induced image of self which is retarding, powerlessness, a sense of alienation from the overall system, unproductive or compensatory consumption, and the many other consequences of poverty.

Of primary importance is the problem of white racism, since it affects every aspect of black life. Its primary manifestation—racial discrimination—prescribes and proscribes black behavioral patterns, customs, aspirations, interpersonal relationships, and economic and political activities and relations. Moreover, it influences black thought processes to such an extent that, until fairly recently, the black American viewed himself through the eyes of white America and, thereby, beheld a self-image which was precisely what white America intended—a view of an inferior being whose badge of inferiority (and shame) was his blackness. Racial discrimination has created a color-caste or ethnic-caste system, reinforced by the legal system, which victimizes blacks and retards black economic development in many ways. As examples, (1) it denies blacks opportunities to share in the affluence of a society which is dependent, in large part, upon the labor and sweat of black people; (2) it results in inequality of access to the necessities for upward socioeconomic mobility; (3) it utilizes blacks, without their consent, as means to ends for whites; and (4) it means "the operation of sanctions which deny blacks access to power, which limit the franchise, sustain job discrimination, permit unequal pay for similar work, or provide inferior training or no training at all."[34]

Chapter Four

Black Economic Development

If economic growth and development are to move forward in an orderly and sound fashion, planning is essential. Planning, in this sense, implies a methodology for moving from one economic state to a different and improved one, or the utilization of rational guidelines to achieve a desired and desirable set of economic objectives. This methodology—these guidelines—must involve an assessment of the current economic situation and its environment, the determination of development goals, the selection of the best means (in terms of action) out of possible alternatives for realizing these goals. It involves the most efficient allocation possible of resources to implement action programs, and requires the direction and coordination of development programs. The fact that the black economy is an economy within an economy does not mean that this methodology or these guidelines are any less essential.

The state of the black economy was the subject of the second chapter. Here, the concern is with the other planning prerequisites listed above.

THE ENVIRONMENT FOR BLACK ECONOMIC DEVELOPMENT[1]

The black economy of the United States is circumscribed and influenced by the national economy of which it is a part. Whatever happens in and to the larger economy has implications for the black economy. Hence, planning for black economic development must take account of basic characteristics and trends in the national economy.

Growth and development of the total economy have been mainly the result of the large and profitable investment opportunities created by a variety of favorable factors and developments. These include the interrelated phenomena of (1) a series of technological discoveries and advances which required heavy capital investments for effective exploitation (e.g., the automobile, the airplane, the computer); (2) the opening up of the West, which provided additional productive resources and made possible the efficient employment of a rapidly increasing population; (3) rapid and sustained urbanization; and (4) the expansion of certain dominant industries—cotton and woolen textiles, the railroad, the automobile, iron and steel—which required huge investments, and which were able to achieve economies of scale because of large and increasing expenditures for consumption—the result, in turn, of a large population (i.e., domestic market). Under these conditions, the opportunities for profitable autonomous investment were such that not only were individual savings readily absorbed, but the expansion of bank credit became increasingly important as a supplemental means of financing needed capital investment.

In the years since World War II, and especially since the 1950s, there have been some rather dramatic changes in these prerequisites for continued economic growth and development—changes so dramatic that not a few economists are beginning to wonder whether the United States economy has neared its potential, in terms of growth and development, and whether what has come to be known as the "stagnation theory" (i.e., the theory which holds that an economy may reach the stage of growth and development when, in the long run, opportunities for profitable investments imply a rate of investment below the rate of savings) may not soon be applicable. For example, consumption expenditures, as a percentage of GNP, decreased from 64.5 percent in 1950 to 62.6 percent in 1972; personal savings during the same period increased from 4.1 percent to 5.6 percent of GNP. If it can be assumed that the majority of personal income—which increased by 133 percent during the period—went mainly to those at the upper end of the income scale, and if it can be further assumed that these changes reflect secular trends, the economy may be facing a condition of diminishing propensity to consume and increasing propensity to save. If, indeed, the economy is facing such a situation, derived investment may not be sufficient to absorb the accumulated savings. Thus, increasing dependence on autonomous investment—that is, investments which result from long-term considerations including technological change, as opposed to derived investments which result from increases in income, sales, and profits—would be necessary. Autonomous investment opportunities appear not to be as great as they have been in the past, because of the decline in the rate of population growth, the disappearance of the Western frontier, and the apparent maturity of a number of dominant industries. This leaves only autonomous investment opportunities the result of technological discoveries and advances. If these opportunities are not sufficient to absorb savings—and it should be pointed out that gross domestic private investment increased only 141 percent during 1960–1972, while personal savings increased by 211 percent—it is likely that the rate of economic growth will decline, unemployment will increase and become more chronic, and the economy will consequently become more stagnant.

It is dangerous to make generalizations and prognoses

on the basis of economic data for a period as short as 1960–1972. However, there are manifestations in the national economy which tend to provide some credibility for the stagnationists. The real rate of growth of the economy for the period 1960–1970 was 4.0 percent, below the rates of growth for that period of all other industrialized countries, except the United Kingdom. Annual real growth rates of output per employee for 1950–1970 and 1960–1970 were 2.1 percent and 2.2 percent respectively—less than the rates experienced in Canada, France, Italy, Japan, the United Kingdom, and West Germany during each of these two periods. The real rate of growth between 1970 and 1971 was 2.7 percent, and between 1971 and 1972, 6.4 percent. During the first three quarters of 1973, the increase in the rate begun in 1972 continued, but available evidence suggests a very sharp decline during the fourth quarter. For example, the industrial production index in December 1973, although 4.5 percent above that of December 1972, was less than that of November 1973, and the annual rate of growth during the fourth quarter of 1973 was 0.9 percent, as compared with 5.5 percent and 6.1 percent, respectively, for the second and third quarters; the decline continued into 1974, amounting to an estimated 1.4 percent by April.[2]

Another especially difficult problem is the one of high and persistent unemployment. Unemployment has dipped to the full employment rate of 4 percent established by the Employment Act of 1946 in only eight years since 1947, and these were the years which coincided with the Korean conflict and the military build-up in Vietnam. In all other years, the rate has ranged from 4.1 percent to 6.8 percent, meaning from 2.8 million to 3.1 million people unemployed. Moreover, the duration of unemployment has increased; for example, those unemployed for fifteen weeks or more during the year increased from 309,000 in 1948 to 1,182,000 in 1971. The particular aspect of unemployment which is of increasing importance is structural unemployment—i.e., unemployment which apparently cannot be effectively combated by the expansion of aggregate demand, and which is causally related to a lack of proper skills and attitudes among and toward the young, the aged, and illiterate, the nonwhites, the residents of depressed areas, and the technologically displaced. These are the hard-core unemployed (to be differentiated from the frictionally and seasonally unemployed)—the unemployed who appear to be immune to any improvement in the overall economic situation—the unemployed who push the rate above the 3–4 percent of the participating labor force which can normally expect to be frictionally or seasonably unemployed in a large and dynamic economy. To a very considerable extent, the structurally unemployed are the unemployables in an economy which is primarily based on the free-enterprise, market system—i.e., where employment and wages are determined by the marginal productivity of labor. The Public Employment Program, authorized by the Emergency Employment Act of 1971, would presumably employ some of these workers in its development of jobs in areas of unmet public needs. At the end of fiscal year 1972, according to the *Manpower Report of the President, 1972*, approximately 160,000 jobs of various kinds throughout the country, funded under the Program, had been filled; the number of unemployed during 1972 averaged 4,840,000 (or a rate of 5.6 percent). The generally upward trend in unemployment, including structural unemployment, suggests that —in the absence of increasing public employment programs —it will become more and more difficult for all able and willing to work in our society to find gainful employment in our society.

Inflation is yet another problem for which a solution is not yet in sight. With $1967=100$, the consumer price index increased from 88.7 in 1960 to 143.1 in March 1974; the wholesale price index increased from 94.9 to 154.5 during the same period. The rate of inflation in the United States is not the highest among the industrialized nations of the world, but this country suffers in comparison with the other industrialized nations in that (1) the index of productivity (i.e., output per man-hour) in the United States is less than that of the other industrialized nations; and (2) except for the United Kingdom, the price level in the United States has increased at a faster rate and that rate is in excess of the rate of increase in productivity. As recently as 1970, a rate of price increase in the neighborhood of 3 percent per year was regarded with concern; now, Americans have become acclimatized to a rate of 6–7 percent. The nature of the inflation is such that economists and policy-makers are baffled, in terms of solutions which will be effective without at the same time decreasing the rate of economic growth and increasing the rate of unemployment beyond tolerable limits. Moreover, the psychological impact of inflation is inflation-reinforcing—the fear of continued inflation produces actions which assure its continuation (and, possibly, acceleration), such as increased capital-spending now in the belief that postponement will mean capital-spending at still higher prices, and the inclusion of cost-of-living escalator clauses in labor contracts based both on past and anticipated increases in the general price level.

Inflation is a major contributing factor to our worsening international economic situation. Manifestations of the international economic problem include, for the period 1960–1972, (1) a transition from an export balance of trade of $4.9 billion to an import balance of $6.8 billion; (2) a surplus on current account of $1.8 billion changing to a deficit of $8 billion; (3) an increase in our basic deficit from $1.2 billion to $9.2 billion; (4) an increase in our net liquidity deficit from $3.7 billion to $14 billion; (5) a growth in our official reserve transactions deficit from $3.4 billion to $10.3 billion (with a deficit of $29.8 billion in 1971); (6) a decrease in the gold stock portion of our international monetary reserves from

$17.9 billion to $10.4 billion (and, it should be noted, our gold stock amounted to $22.9 billion in 1950); and (7) a depreciation of the value of our currency with respect to the currencies of all other industrialized nations. Domestic inflation and greater increases in productivity abroad, it should be emphasized, are not the sole contributing factors to our worsened international economic situation—also of importance are (1) the transition of the United States to the status of a mature creditor nation (where dividends, interest and repayments from our past investments abroad tend to be greater than our new investments abroad and, thus, produce the effect of an excess of imports over exports); (2) our large economic and military assistance programs abroad; (3) an erosion of international confidence in the United States dollar; and (4) the increasing importance of nonexportable services in our GNP.

Exacerbating the problems of growth, unemployment, inflation, and our balance of international payments are shortages in areas which are extremely critical with reference to all these problems. Shortages of oil and of certain foodstuffs and grains have been sufficiently publicized to obviate the need for discussion here.

This, then, is a picture of the national economy, of which the black economy is an integral part. It is not a picture which provides maximum encouragement and stimulation to the development and improvement of the black economy. And, yet, within the limitations imposed by the national economy, black economic expansion and improvement can go forward.

BLACK ECONOMIC GOALS

Economic development involves both economic and noneconomic change. In terms of the concerns of this chapter, this means that it is necessary to direct planning for black economic development in such a way that there is a minimization of friction with noneconomic phenomena, while achieving a maximization of beneficial economic change. Thus, the goals of black economic development—as is true for any economic development—must include changes in attitudes, institutions, human skills, information availabilities, as well as economic changes. Moreover, many of the economic factors and forces which must be changed have noneconomic as well as economic bases; black poverty, discussed at length in the preceding chapter, is an excellent example which underscores this point.

The goals of black economic development must be (1) a closing of the gaps between blacks and whites regarding all the indicators of economic well-being; (2) a more equitable distribution of income within the black community; and (3) increased upward mobility for black people. These are not mutually exclusive, but extremely interrelated and interdependent, goals.

With particular reference to the disparity in income, an important cause of income distribution is the ownership of wealth. Statistics on black ownership of wealth are practically nonexistent. It is possible, however, to make some deductions from the statistics which are available. Robert Lampman, professor of economics at the University of Wisconsin, has perhaps studied wealth distribution in the United States as much as any economist. He concludes that about 20 percent of the wealth of the country is owned by the public. Of the remaining wealth—i.e., that owned by the personal sector of the economy—more than 30 percent in 1953 was owned by 1.6 percent of the total adult population. This "group owned at least 80 percent of the corporate stock, virtually all of the state and local government bonds, and between 10 and 33 percent of each other type of property in the personal sector in that year."[3] Relatively few blacks are in this group. Dorothy Projector and Gertrude Weiss, staff economists in the division of research and statistics, Board of Governors of the Federal Reserve completed a study of the distribution of wealth in 1962. One of their conclusions was that "There is a strong positive relation between size of wealth and size of current income. Average wealth is estimated to be about $7600 for consumer units with incomes less than $3000 and is larger for each successive income level, reaching well over $1,000,000 for those with incomes of $100,000 or more."[4] In 1969, 92 percent of nonwhite families had annual incomes of less than $15,000, which is a severe limitation to the acquisition of wealth.

In addition to the accumulation of wealth out of income, the other main method of acquisition is through wealth transfers, usually inheritance. Again, the absence of reliable statistics constitutes a handicap, but it can be assumed that the amount of transferred wealth between blacks is insignificant. One limitation on the availability of wealth which could be transferred is the fact that whites have systematically managed to acquire from blacks much of the wealth they have managed to acquire.[5]

The gaps in income within the black community are critical to black economic development. The gaps are suggested by the following statistics on the distribution of nonwhite families by annual income in 1947, 1960, and 1969:[6]

TABLE 14

Nonwhite Annual Income

Income	1947	1960	1969
Number of families (thousands)	3117	4333	5215
Under $3,000	57%	38%	20%
$ 3,000–$ 4,999	25	22	19
$ 5,000–$ 6,999	9	16	17
$ 7,000–$ 9,999	6	14	20
$10,000–$14,999	3	7	16
$15,000 and over	0	2	8
	100%	100%	100%

Although greater equality of income was experienced during the period, significant gaps remained. To be sure, gaps in income will always exist in a system in which income is a function of the marginal productivities of productive factors. This, however, is not an adequte argument against pursuing means of maximally closing these gaps.

In the mid-1960s, Professors Eli Ginzberg and Dale Heisand, of Columbia University, were requested by the U.S. Civil Rights Commission to delineate those factors that impeded the upward socioeconomic mobility of minority groups, and especially blacks, in our society. They concluded that upward mobility is a function of employment, income, education, and standard of living.[7] These prerequisites for upward mobility constitute the poverty syndrome, which applies so specifically to blacks—the standard of living depends upon income, which depends upon employment, which depends upon education, which depends upon the standard of living. At which point of this vicious circle is meaningful intervention effected? One approach is based largely on the theory that people are poor because they do not have money and, therefore, all that is needed to terminate poverty is to give money to those in poverty. The history of welfare programs, in terms of lifting people out of poverty, is replete with examples of dismal failures, for several reasons. First, the amount of money usually provided has never been enough to provide for the poor even decent minimum standards of living. Second, the manner in which the welfare programs have been administered tends to degrade the welfare recipient, with adverse psychological consequences. Third, instead of getting at the root causes of poverty, the programs have tended to perpetuate poverty.

ACHIEVING THE GOALS OF BLACK ECONOMIC DEVELOPMENT

About ten years ago, after the 1964 Supreme Court decision outlawing segregated education (Brown v. the Board of Education), a wave of optimism swept over the country regarding the enhanced prospects for black human and economic development. For example, the publication of the prestigious American Academy of Political and Social Science was moved to state that, "The effect thus far, both of the organized [black] protest movement and of the social change operating throughout American society, has been to bring about changes generally in accord with the major goals of the [black protest] movement,"[8] although it was recognized that blacks may not share in that optimism and that new forces may develop which would prolong the complete victory of the black protest movement. In that same publication, certain economic forces were foreseen as operating which would serve the ends of the black protest movement. These forces included rising urban employment and wage rates in the South that would benefit blacks, nondiscriminatory employment opportunities in government for blacks, and the success of black purchasing power in pressing for nondiscriminatory employment policies among employers.[9] Unfortunately, almost ten years later, progress on these fronts has been limited.

People conceive of reality in terms of their own sense of values, which are conditioned by their cultural, intellectual, and experiential backgrounds and development. Black Americans are not a homogeneous population in terms of either background or development. Hence, opinions on the reality of black economic development, and the means for attaining that reality, will vary. That on which all blacks will undoubtedly agree is that planned change is essential for black economic development—that on which there will be great disagreement is the most effective means of achieving planned change (e.g., integration v. separation, or individual v. community ownership and control of business and other economic activities).

Whatever the means chosen, black economic development must involve qualitative as well as quantitative changes. The qualitative changes are the more difficult to effect, because they presuppose an evolutionary—or revolutionary—process encompassing structural alterations, consideration of and coping with an array of noneconomic factors, intervention in the development process, and rationalized planning and goal-determination. The black community is a subculture within the larger American culture. As such, it exists within an environment of beliefs, customs, and values reflecting patterns of behavior which differ—in some instances very markedly—from the beliefs, customs and values of the majority culture. Hence, the necessity arises for altering developmental techniques to fit the peculiar situation of the black community, and for developing an appropriate combination of programs based upon these techniques.

As an absolute minimum, programs for achieving the above-stated goals must include increased quality and diversification of the labor force, more effective utilization of manpower, assurances of decent living standards in the absence of earning capacity, improved consumer knowledge, increased wealth accumulation, expanded and improved business enterprise. The last prerequisite—entrepreneurship—is of sufficient importance to warrant special treatment; the succeeding chapter deals with it in considerable detail. The other prerequisites for achieving the goals of black economic development are discussed here.

1. Increased Quality and Diversification of the Labor Force

The ultimate objective of efforts directed towards this end is the advancement of black economic development and welfare while, at the same time, enhancing for the individual, possibilities of job mobility, fulfillment of potential, and work satisfaction. The major responsibility for accomplishing this objective falls on the educational system, but government, employers, and unions must also play their proper roles.

Clifton R. Wharton, Jr., president of Michigan State University, concludes that "Black intellectual manpower is the human capital indispensable to black economic development and social progress.... If the black economy is to prosper, if black society is to forge ahead, if our black people are to flourish, we must strengthen and expand our base of intellectual power."[10] With respect to the diversification of this intellectual power, he states further that "there is the challenge of moving black students away from the fields which have been traditional for blacks, such as education, and into neglected fields, such as science. This is not to disparage the need for qualified teachers but to highlight the need to encourage and attract black youth into other areas—such as engineering, business, criminology, communications, physics, biochemistry, and statistics. They must acquire marketable skills which lead to positions of influence and power."[11]

Black economic growth and development, if it is to be enduring, must rely on a greater supply of competent men and women in areas and disciplines that heretofore have been largely foreign to blacks, as well as on competent people in the traditionally black professions. This has particular implications for the predominantly black colleges—they must, with the admittedly inadequate funds available to them, reappraise their objectives and reorient their curricula more in terms of what is happening in the real world. The traditional liberal-arts approach to education no longer suffices for today's world of work—it does not enhance the possibilities for individual fulfillment in terms of socially interesting, intellectually demanding, and economically rewarding employment and careers. On the other hand, an overemphasis on relevant education can result in shallow intellectualism, unwarranted elitism, and other problems. Somehow, black higher education must find that happy middle ground where black youth are educated for meaningful participation and rewarding contributions in an increasingly technical and complex world while, at the same time, they are not denied the undeniable benefits of a well-rounded education. If the predominantly black colleges are to discharge this obligation for the intellectual development of black people—if they are to continue to develop black leaders—they must be assisted financially and increasingly by government—both federal and state—and by corporations, since previous sources of funding (i.e., religious organizations, foundations, and wealthy persons) appear to be losing interest in black institutions of higher education.[12]

Whether or not such financial assistance is forthcoming, the predominantly black schools can add strength and variety to their programs through more cooperative endeavors with the predominantly white institutions of higher education. At least two programs, now operating on a relatively small scale, should be expanded. One of these involves the utilization of the faculty members of white schools to teach courses, conduct seminars, and otherwise participate in the instructional activities of the black schools.[13] Not only should this program be expanded to include both more schools and individual curricula, but maximum utilization of black faculty members of white schools should be effected. The other program is the development of more arrangements which will permit students of black schools to take courses at the white institutions without additional charge. The arrangement could be effected by cross-registration or some other device.[14] A particularly attractive variation of this program is one in which a black student in a black school follows for three years a course of study previously agreed upon by pertinent faculty members and administrators at that school and at a cooperating predominantly white institution, after which he enrolls in the predominantly white school for an additional two years (taking whatever courses as are still necessary at the black school). At the end of the five years, the students are awarded a bachelor's degree from the black school and a master's degree from the white school, thus effecting a usual saving of a year while being exposed to a greatly enriched learning experience.[15]

Yet another means of enriching the educational offerings of black colleges is through cooperative programs with business and industrial corporations. This cooperation can take various forms, which are not mutually exclusive. The two most common are (a) cooperative work-study programs, whereby students work for corporations—during summers, a semester and/or a year—while still enrolled in school, and (b) the use of corporate personnel as part-time faculty members.[16]

Not all black students pursuing higher education are to be found in the predominantly black colleges, of course. In 1970, of the 522,000 blacks enrolled in institutions of higher education, 72.4 percent were enrolled in predominantly white institutions.[17] Despite their greater financial resources, richer curricula, larger faculties, and better educational facilities and equipment, the predominantly white schools have had their own unique set of problems in the preparation of their increasing black enrollees for the world of work. Clifton Wharton has summarized these as "the lack of prior preparation or planning for such students and the absence of prior experience with students from such backgrounds. Poor orientation, inadequate support services, insufficient black staff and professors . . . personal and social difficulties arising between black and white students, whose cultural values or 'life-styles' are often significantly different."[18] Wharton goes on to add, "There are three major academic challenges facing predominantly white institutions—to provide the black student with viable career choices, to offer him a relevant education, and to help him survive financial constraints."[19] Many of the predominantly white institutions are serious in meeting these challenges; others, however, have elected to bow to the unreasoned demands of black students for such educational pursuits as black studies curricula, which provide little in the way of marketable skills upon graduation. By thus "copping out," these latter institutions are providing a disservice to their black students in terms of employment and career potentials.

Institutions of higher education cannot be assigned the

full responsibility for the education of black youth—efforts to assure quality education at the elementary and secondary levels must be intensified. In view of the long history of inferior education for blacks under a "separate but equal" system, this means complete desegregation of schools and programs. In 1970, there were 6,707,400 black elementary and secondary students enrolled in schools. Despite the fact that administrators of the educational systems had had sixteen years to implement the Supreme Court's decision on school desegregation, 66.9 percent (4,483,900) of these students were enrolled in schools in which the total enrollment was 50 to 100 percent black, 38.2 percent (2,563,300) were in schools in which the enrollment was 95 to 100 percent black, and 14.0 percent (941,100) were in schools in which the total enrollment was black.[20] The inferior quality of education to be found in all-black or predominantly black schools —the result of gross inadequacies in financing—is well-documented. The consequences of the inferior quality of education include generally lower achievement test scores for blacks than for whites, the greater likelihood that black teenagers will be enrolled in grades below modal grades for their age than whites, the less likelihood that blacks will complete secondary school and go on to college than whites, and the consequently greater handicaps which blacks have when they enter the labor force and compete for employment.

For those blacks already a part of the labor force—many of whom are unemployed or underemployed—special programs are necessary to produce or increase marketable knowledge and skills. These programs must be designed to compensate for past and present lacks of access to equal educational and work-experience opportunities. Thus, these programs must be essentially different from and improvements on past manpower development programs. In 1969, when blacks accounted for approximately 11 percent of the labor force, they accounted for only about 7.5 percent of those participating in adult education and manpower development and training programs.[21] It is in this area that the need for cooperation between educational institutions (at all levels), government, unions, and employers, in programs designed to upgrade and diversify the black labor force, is most essential.[22]

2. More Effective Utilization of Manpower

The manner in which employed manpower is utilized has important implications for economic development. Everett Hagen, the M.I.T. economist, observes that economic growth and development are accompanied by increased ratios of capital inputs to labor inputs (Table 15), increased divisions of labor among and within productive units (Table 16), and a greater increase in the average value of output per worker first in secondary industry over primary industry and then in tertiary industry over primary industry, with consequent shifts in the distribution of the labor force (Table 1).[23] In the United States as a whole during the post-World War II period, for example, these changes are most notable, as shown by the following statistics:

TABLE 15

Changed Ratio of Productive Inputs[24]

	1950	1970	Percentage Change
Gross private domestic investment in nonresidential structures and producers' durable equipment, in billions of dollars (base 1967 = 100)	44.1	85.0	94.8%
Employed manpower (millions)	58.9	78.6	33.4%

Changes in the distribution of the nonwhite labor force, however, have been far less notable, as shown by the statistics on nonwhites as a percentage of all workers in selected

TABLE 16

Changes in Production as between Primary,
Secondary and Tertiary Industries,
in Billions of Dollars, at 1958 Prices[25]

Year	Primary Industry (i)	Secondary Industry (ii)	Tertiary Industry (iii)
1950	$20.4	$121.7	$165.3
1955	22.1	154.4	201.1
1960	23.1	162.6	238.0
1968	24.6	244.4	352.0

(i) Agriculture, forestry, and fisheries
(ii) Manufacturing, mining, and construction
(iii) Transportation, communications, trade, finance, insurance, real estate, and other services (excluding government)

occupations for 1960 and 1970. (See Table 2; page 19.) In 1970, as before, there was a concentration of nonwhite workers in the low-paying service labor and farm occupations, as shown by Table 3 (see page 19).

A serious obstacle to more effective utilization of the black labor force is the historically discriminatory actions of craft unions. Through the various regulatory devices available to these unions for controlling apprenticeships, the entrance of blacks into the building construction, electrical, plumbing, mechanical, metal, printing, and other high-income trades has been effectively and severely limited. For example, in 1972, only 6 percent of the almost 300,000 apprentices were black; this represented a substantial increase as compared with five years earlier. This black percentage was not spread evenly over the apprenticeship-controlling craft unions, however, since the proportions in the electrical, plumbing, and mechanical trades were only 2–3 percent.[26] Even if, somehow, blacks develop skills in these trades by means other than apprenticeships, the closed-shop provisions in contracts negotiated by these unions—or conspiratorial agreements between the unions and employers—are barriers to black employment in these trades. The expectations for changes in this situation, engendered by the "Philadelphia Plan" programs (i.e., programs to increase the proportions of black workers on construction projects financed, totally or partially, by federal funds) of the U.S. Department of Labor, have not been significantly realized.[27]

There has been no dearth of announced programs to improve the utilization of black manpower. Many leading business enterprises have programs—at least on paper—for hiring, training, and developing minority managerial and technical personnel. Plans for Progress and the National Alliance of Business represent cooperative efforts on the part of corporations to enhance the employment and advancement possibilities for black and other minority employees. The Equal Employment Opportunity Commission, with a Congressional mandate to effect equal employment and advancement opportunities for minorities, has worked diligently to discharge its responsibility. Despite these programs—and the "law of the land," as contained in Section III of the Civil Rights Act of 1964—progress has been disappointingly slow. There are several reasons for the discouraging results thus far, most of which are related to continuing racial discrimination in employment and advancement—the resistance, lack of interest, and other negative attitudes of entrenched front-line managers and supervisors; the lack of effective leadership and direction in top levels of management; outmoded and often illegal employment and advancement criteria; inadequate and ineffective organizational orientation, motivation, counseling, and assimilation programs; archaic and inflated views of the nature of the work to be performed (often deliberately conceived to screen out black employees); and the continued racially exclusionary policies and practices of some labor unions.

The increased employment of blacks in managerial positions by the corporate world in recent years is deserving of special mention within this context. Many of these new managers have become concerned for two reasons—i.e., (a) the lack of opportunities for the full development of their managerial potential, and (b) the fact that, as they look down the corporate ladder from whatever position they hold, they see few or no other blacks moving up. This concern has resulted in a concerted action on the part of some of these black managers, with the encouragement and assistance of sympathetic white management personnel, which is noteworthy. On February 8, 1971, the Association for the Integration of Management (AIM), Inc., was established. The overall objective of AIM is "the achievement of full participation in management." Organized for "the express purpose of developing a systematic approach to the elimination of racism in the management structure of American business corporations," AIM has specific objectives which include (1) accelerated advancement of current and potential black managers into key management positions and significant leadership roles in the major corporations; (2) informing the public, the government and the business community about the underutilization of blacks in management, and working with the business community to remedy same; (3) encouragement, assistance, and guidance of black youth in their efforts to begin management careers; (4) the exploration and development of solutions to the problems arising out of the confrontation of the white business community and its values by the black subculture and its values; and (5) the design of specific management development and career guidance programs to meet the special needs of black managerial aspirants.

It is clear that more vigorous enforcement of existing nondiscriminatory legislation and regulations is necessary if an effective and efficient utilization of black manpower is to be realized. The interim report of the American Assembly on "The Changing World of Work," referred to earlier, makes the following pertinent observation: "Our progress is significant only in contrast to where we were a decade ago. We must develop a more effective national effort to achieve opportunity for full participation in the work force at all levels of employment."[28] Racial and social equality and justice aside, a better utilization of black manpower makes economic sense in that it would result in a larger national product for all of society.

3. Assurances of Decent Living Standards

The evidence is increasingly strong that this economy, short of war, cannot provide employment for everyone who is able and willing to work in our society. The evidence is equally strong that, in this situation, black members of the labor force are among those hardest hit by unemployment. The very serious problem which emerges from the inability to earn an income, or an income which is sufficient to assure standards of living which are decent and adequate in terms of criteria established by our society, is that of developing measures whereby socially acceptable standards of living are assured in the absence of earned income.

About a decade ago, many Americans were outraged at the suggestion that people in our society should receive income whether they work or not—that they should be paid to live. The reaction to this suggestion might have been considerably different—perhaps the suggestion would have been ignored or dismissed as the unrealistic musings of extreme radicalists—if it had not come from a group of respected and reputable American citizens who had gathered at the equally respected and reputable Center for Democratic Studies (in Santa Barbara, California) to ponder some of the socioeconomic ills besetting the country. The report containing this suggestion—The Triple Revolution—carried further many of the concerns of Michael Harrington's *The Other America*, generally credited with spotlighting for the first time the realities of abject poverty in our affluent society. The concerns and suggestions were not ignored or dismissed, however, and despite misinterpretations and criticisms, the sown seeds began to bear fruit. For example, support for a negative income tax developed in sources from which such support would have been unthinkable only a few years before.

There can be no doubt about the ability of our economy to provide each and every American with an adequate and decent standard of living. The problem is the will to do so. Closely coupled with this will is the means of doing so, i.e., if the means could be developed and largely accepted, the will would be forthcoming. Of necessity, what is at issue is some more advanced form of income redistribution than has yet been attempted. In a society such as ours—characterized by unprecedented affluence, and gross inequalities in the distribution of income (and wealth)—income redistribution has both moral and social appeal. Moreover, at least two strong economic arguments are possible for a more equal distribution of income—(a) increased income to blacks (and other minorities), many of whom of necessity have a high propensity to consume, might have a greater multiplier effect on national income than is likely to obtain under the present distribution; and (b) societal satisfaction might be maximized—the goal of utilitarian economic philosophy—by redistribution, since taking from the haves will result in a loss of satisfaction which is less than the increase in satisfaction resulting from giving to the have nots. On the other hand, income redistribution could have some undesirable consequences. For example, it might (a) adversely affect economic growth and development, since these are dependent on some people in society having more income than they need with the excess being available for the economic growth and development preconditions of savings and investment; (b) increase to an undesirable extent the economic role of government not only because of the need to administer the redistribution but also because of the possible necessity for government to take up the investment slack in the interest of continued growth and development; (c) have the effect of a net decrease in societal satisfaction since some activities now supported by the richer members of society and considered desirable by many members of society—e.g., certain cultural activities—may no longer be funded; and (d) result in undesirable economic dislocations as a result of shifts in demands for some commodities and services.

Income redistribution of the magnitude necessary to assure an adequate and decent standard of living to those with incomes below an acceptable poverty level—to include the full-time working poor—will be costly. But, as Robert Lampman has observed in *Poverty in America,* the existence of poverty is itself costly—costly in terms of the poor's very small contribution to the national product, in terms of transfer payments (unemployment compensation, public welfare, etc.), in terms of increased costs to society for various types of protection (fire, police and health), in terms of a smaller tax base than would otherwise be the case, and in terms of societal tensions.[29] Taking these costs and the two possible salutary economic consequences above into consideration, the justification for a more effective income-redistribution program is very strong. Moreover, there are undoubtedly economic and other knowledge and skills available for the formulation and implementation of the type of program required so that the possibilities of the four adverse consequences, mentioned above, are minimized or eliminated.

4. Improved Consumer Knowledge

The exploitation of black consumers has been documented by various studies. For example, the National Advisory Commission of Civil Disorders found that "significant grievances concerning unfair commercial practices affecting (black) consumers were found in 11 of the 20 cities studied by the Commission."[30] David Caplovitz in *The Poor Pay More* documents various forms of cheating by merchants. These include the misrepresentation of the prices of goods, the substitution of inferior goods for those ordered, the sale of reconditioned products as new, bait advertising, and switch sales.[31] The Federal Trade Commission, in its concern about deception in the sale of goods on installment plans, found that in Washington, D.C., in 1966, (a) the average gross margin on durable goods sold by low-income-market retailers ranged from nine to twenty-eight percentage points higher than that charged by general-market furniture stores; (b) the gross margin, as a percentage of sales, was 61 percent for low-income-market retailers, as compared with 37 percent for general-market retailers; (c) the retail price differences on durable goods between low-income-market retailers and general-market retailers ranged from $14.95 for an Admiral portable television to $150 for an Admiral dryer; and (d) the gross profit margin for low-income-market retailers was 62.2 percent, as compared with 35.5 percent for general-market retailers.[32] Statistics developed by the Bureau of the Census reveal that black homeowners are more likely to have loans which are a larger percentage of the purchase price (and, thus, require larger monthly payments) than white homeowners, that black homeowners pay higher interest rates than white homeowners, that the purchase price for black homeowners tends to be higher than for white homeowners for comparable housing, that a smaller percentage of black homeowners have government-assisted loans than white homeowners, and that a much larger percentage of black homeowners have loans of relatively short duration than do white homeowners.[33] A series of articles in the *Washington Post*, a few years ago, exposed fairly typical and deplorably unethical practices of real estate speculators in the matter of housing for blacks. Because of inability to obtain credit from conventional sources, many black Washingtonians—and this is also true for residents in other areas—were (and still are) victimized by second, third, and even, fourth mortgages held by these speculators; by speculators buying houses at one price and selling them to blacks two or three months later with fairly common mark-ups of 25 to 50 percent without any improvements being made on the property; by extortionate "lease-purchase" arrangements; and by other despicable practices.[34]

The consumption patterns of blacks are motivated by factors which make them easy prey for exploitative practices and policies. These factors include a history of deprivation of basic necessities, desire to compensate for past deprivations and current blocked socioeconomic mobility, basic unfamiliarities with the urban culture, residential restrictions which lock blacks into the urban ghetto or into dilapidated "across-the-tracks" residential areas in nonurban settings, inadequate public transportation into and out of their restricted residential areas, the ease of unethical installment-buying and other usurious forms of credit, and a lack of education and training which would make them effective consumers in a bureaucratic society. Under this set of circumstances, markups of 100 percent or more on low-quality goods, reconditioned furniture and appliances sold as new, excessively adverse credit terms, and other examples of customer exploitation, are the usual means of doing business. Under such a combination of circumstances, repossessions, garnishments, property attachments, and bad or nonexistent credit ratings tend to impoverish even more an already impoverished minority.

Price elasticity of demand is a determining factor in the exploitability of black consumers. In view of some of the factors listed above—specifically, residential restrictions, inadequate public transportation, unfamiliarity with the urban culture, and the lack of pertinent education and training—black demand for many consumer goods is less than elastic as far as area retailers are concerned. Hence, regardless of price—or quality or attendant services—these retailers are able to depend on continued sales to a captive market. Consumer education programs designed to increase the elasticity of black demand for consumption goods—as one other means of increasing the economic well-being of blacks and thereby serving the ends of black economic development—are urgently needed. Such programs should not be limited to food, clothing, and housing but should cover medical care, legal services, insurance, consumer financing, and all other "competitors" for black consumer dollars. The number of organizations—both public and private, and including especially educational institutions—which can assist in the formulation and implementation of consumer education programs is steadily increasing.

5. Increased Accumulation of Wealth

The accumulation of wealth is possible from one or a combination of four processes—i.e., returns on previously accumulated wealth, an effective utilization of debt, the conversion of income into wealth, and wealth transfers. Of these, the last two appear to offer the greatest potential for blacks.

The potential of converting income into wealth depends upon the ability to earn more income than is necessary for current consumption. Education, skill development, employment opportunities, and advancement possibilities are the major determinants of black income, but—as has been shown—racially discriminatory policies and practices in each of these areas are severe limitations to the earning of that income. Additionally, as has also been shown, the exploitation of black consumers by unethical sellers of goods and services results in more of black income going into consumption than would be the case if equality in consumption opportunities existed.

Despite these deterrents to capital accumulation, there is reason to believe that the volume of savings among blacks may be larger than generally supposed—although certainly not large enough to finance the magnitude of black economic development required. In support of this belief are the results of several studies which conclude that (a) given the same income, blacks tend to spend less on consumption than do whites, (b) relatively low-income blacks average less debt than do whites with comparable incomes, and (c) middle-income blacks average larger net increases in savings than do middle-income whites.[35] Two comments on these conclusions seem warranted—(a) a major reason for less debt among low-income blacks may be their greater difficulty in obtaining credit, and (b) the greater savings among middle-income blacks may be partially the result of resistance to the indignities of racial discrimination in attempting to spend their disposable income, and partially the result of the realization that more overt and/or covert racial discrimination could overnight plunge them into the poverty from which they are only one step removed.

An indication of the magnitude of the conversion of black income into wealth is possible from statistics on the assets of black banks, savings and loan companies, and insurance companies. It is an indication only, because (a) not all black savings go into black institutions, and (b) there is some degree of nonblack savings in each of these three types of black institutions. The statistics for 1972 were:[36]

TABLE 17

Black Business

Institutions	Number	Assets
Banks	37	$ 652,262,110
Savings & Loan Associations	44	456,990,724
Life Insurance Companies	44	494,731,801
Total		$1,603,984,635

The total assets of these institutions, it should be emphasized, were about $30 million less than those of Allied Chemical, the sixty-fifth ranking corporation in *Fortune Magazine's* 500 largest corporations in 1972.[37] The total assets of the banks were less than 30 percent of the assets of the fiftieth ranking commercial bank—Security National Bank of Hempstead, New York—in the country in that year, and the total assets of the life insurance companies were about $80 million less than those of the fiftieth ranking life insurance company —Kansas City Life.[38]

There have been some notable examples of black wealth-accumulation successes outside the black financial institutions. These include the "10–36" (i.e., $10 per person per week for 36 weeks) plan of the Reverend Leon Sullivan and his church in Philadelphia, which led to the construction of apartment complexes, a shopping center, and several thriving manufacturing establishments. The shopping center and other business activities in St. Louis, initially conceived by James Hurt and made possible by the willingness of black ministers and their churches to cooperate in making the conception a reality are another example. Finally, the mobilization of funds and consequent rapidly expanding economic activities of the Black Muslims are still another. The list could be extended and all these activities are to be highly commended. Their successes, apparently the only means of attaining the goals outlined earlier in this chapter, are nonetheless limited.

It is obvious that black economic development, on the scale necessary, is impossible if it must rely solely on accumulated wealth possibilities in the black community. The black stock must be augmented with wealth from outside the black community—and this means wealth transfers. Several proposals for such transfers have been made during the past several years, including suggestions (and requests) for reparation payments for past discrimination and "short-changing." The proposal which appeals to the present author most—because it addresses itself to the root cause of black powerlessness in and black alienation from the economic mainstream of our society—is the one made by Richard America in the *Harvard Business Review* a few years ago.[39] Essentially, and briefly, America suggests a transfer of some major national corporations to black ownership and control, through a mechanism by which the government would compensate current owners commensurate with market or negotiated values for their equities, and would provide for the resale of these equities to blacks at prices very considerably below acquisition costs with the government absorbing the difference. America cites public-interest precedents for his proposal, including government assistance in the opening up of the West; the transfer of technology from public to private hands; commercialization of the results of government financed research and development; and the federal urban renewal program involving the acquisition of property by the government through the exercise of eminent domain and the subsequent resale after improvements are made on the property to developers at a fraction of the total cost. The proposal envisages the transfer of about 125 of the country's largest manufacturing and other corporations to black ownership and control—i.e., about eight corporations a year for fifteen years, at which time "the procedure would be discontinued since by then blacks will have achieved economic parity roughly equivalent to their proportion of the population."

MANAGING BLACK ECONOMIC DEVELOPMENT

It is assumed that there will be general agreement that the implementation of black economic development programs should be directed toward (1) maximum efficiency in the utilization of human, financial, and other resources; (2) the achievement of the fullest employment possible of these resources; (3) the expansion of, and improvement in, the flow of goods and services produced by these resources; (4) maximum equity in the distribution of income resulting from the employment of these resources; and (5) minimum economic and financial instability during the development process. There is considerable conflict between some of these objectives, in that more of one usually means less of some other. Thus, there must be choices between them which should represent conscious trade-offs, with due consideration of the consequences of alternative trade-offs. If deliberate and conscious trade-offs do not constitute the basis for development policy, then policy will be determined on an ad hoc basis, *but there must be a development policy!* It is the job of management to choose between these alternatives, and to formulate and implement development policy. This management, if it is to be effective and efficient, must be constituted by "individuals with entrepreneurial spirit and energy, who are innovative, who have the capacity for translating ideas into action, who are receptive to change and are initiators of change, who have a high tolerance for ambiguity and uncertainty, and who have the will to risk."[40] It is instructive to analyze the meaning of this quotation from the point of view of the requirements for black economic development.

Entrepreneurship—the entrepreneurial spirit—occupies a unique place in economic development. Joseph A. Schumpeter viewed it as the "fundamental phenomenon of economic development," in that it is essential for the carrying out of the new combinations of the means of production which are necessarily implied in the development process.[41] The entrepreneur is to be distinguished from the inventor, the disseminator of knowledge, and the financier, so far as economic development is concerned. Although variously defined, in economic development literature, entrepreneurship is herein understood to mean the ability to perceive new opportunities for benefit or gain and the willingness to exploit them—it describes the type of person whose attitudes and capabilities are such that he positively initiates action, innovatively organizes resources, and creatively achieves goals.[42]

Innovation, again according to Schumpeterian analysis, is also an essential ingredient in economic development. It is defined as the commercial or industrial application of a new product, process, form of organization or combination of existing productive resources. The innovator is to be distinguished from the inventor, who discovers the new "thing," and the capitalist who finances the innovation, although the innovation, invention, and financing may all be the product of the same person. It is the innovator, thus, who "introduces the devices that save time, labor, and cost. He opens the new markets. He tries out the new management techniques."[43] If an economy is to grow and develop, innovative activity must be encouraged. Whereas entrepreneurship is essential for the carrying out of the new combinations of the means of production, innovation *is* the carrying out of such new combinations. Innovation, thus, may involve (a) the introduction of a new good or a new quality of a good; (b) the introduction of a new method of production; (c) the opening up of a new market; (d) the development of a new source of supply for raw materials or semi-manufactured goods; and/or (e) the carrying out of a new organization of industry.[44]

Innovative behavior, at the individual level, consists of six sequential stages—i.e., the configuration of ideas, the recombination of ideas, the identification of relevant new ideas, the substitution of old ideas, the discrimination between different ideas, and the final evaluation of losses and gains associated with different ideas. This analysis of innovative behavior reveals a dependence upon many qualities that are emotional and psychological in nature and, hence, may be innate to the individual.[45] These qualities, however, can be greatly enhanced by analytical ability, especially with respect to environmental factors, and mastery in pertinent cognitive areas. Both the analytical ability and cognitive knowledge must be acquired from management education and training processes.

The capability of translating ideas into action presupposes a mixture of managerial and entrepreneurial qualities. Some of these are innate to the individual, many of which can be enhanced with proper education and training. Others must be developed by education and training. A list of such qualities includes aggressiveness, self-confidence, communications skill, independence, self-reliance, leadership, persuasiveness, decisiveness, the ability to accept loss and hostility from others, creativity and, of course, technical knowledge and skills.

Receptivity to and the capability of initiating change is especially important for economic development. The process of development involves social change and development; political, governmental, and institutional change; economic change and modernization; and structural and process changes. In short, the very essence of economic development is change, especially qualitative change, and there can be no economic development without it. Despite the necessity of change in order for economic development to proceed, adaptation to change—and, even less, anticipation and initiation of change—is fraught with difficulties in most developing situations.

George M. Foster, in his study of technological change in developing countries, observed that "Cultural, social and psychological barriers and stimulants to change exist in an economic setting. In a more comprehensive analysis, economic factors should receive extensive treatment, for they seem to set the absolute limits to change. People are often unwilling to change their ways, because of cultural and social and psychological factors. But equally as often, they are quite aware of the value of change and anxious to alter their traditional ways, but the economic sacrifice is too great. If an economic potential does not exist or cannot be built into a program of directed change, the most careful attention to culture and society will be meaningless."[46] Barriers to change, which somehow must be overcome, are classifiable as (a) cultural (e.g., values, attitudes, and cultural structure); (b) social (e.g., group solidarity, conflict, loci of authority, and characteristics of the social structure); and (c) psychological (e.g., differential perceptions, communication problems, and learning problems).

One of the major qualifications for modern management is a high tolerance for ambiguity and uncertainty. K. J. Davey, in his study of decision-making in East Africa, observed that uncertainty is a crucial factor, and that there are three types of uncertainty—uncertainty over different perceptions of values, uncertainty over related decisions of colleagues within one's organization, and uncertainties over the external environment.[47] Ambiguity and uncertainty constitute risk. If the ideal model of decision-making is examined, it is usually in the third stage—i.e., the identification of alternative methods for solving problems and the choice of the alternative with the most advantageous cost-benefit ratio— that the greatest risk (ambiguity and uncertainty) is encountered. True, the identification of the problem and need for a decision—the first stage—involves individual judgments which make a specific problem appear differently to different people; thus, the need for a decision, as well as the decision itself, will also tend to differ. Stage two—or the choice of objectives—likewise is confusion-prone, because of the conflict between values and facts. Stages four (implementation), five (monitoring progress), and six (review of progress and modification of objectives) may also involve some ambiguity and uncertainty, but they are relatively minor.

Risk is associated with variability—the more variable the expected outcome, the riskier the decision. Thus, risk can be defined in terms of probability distributions of possible results—the more widespread the distribution, the greater the variability, and the higher the risk. Since it is not possible to forecast the future with exact precision, all decision-making involves some risk. It is usually the risk-taker rather than the risk-averter, however, who is generally handed the accolades for success in management. This is not the result of the fact that the risk-taker is a bigger gambler, but because the risk-taker is more familiar with the techniques used to structure problems and to generate data necessary for optimization analysis. These techniques, which facilitate decision-making under conditions of ambiguity and uncertainty, are not intuitive in nature—they must be acquired and mastered, often only as a result of rigorous study and application.

The complex task of managing development requires an integrated and multi-disciplinary approach. This means, first of all, abandoning the assumption that certain types of management are so unique that they must be separated and taught in conceptually different ways—separate and distinct conceptualizations for government, business, education, health care. Secondly, it means abandoning the traditional assumption that there is a prevailing set of ideas to approach rationally organizational problems in any culture. Once having put these two assumptions to rest, the task of managing black economic development then becomes one of strengthening managerial capacity by improving the knowledge, skills, and attitudes of managers; by better selection and utilization of managerial talent; by the introduction of better managerial techniques; and by changes in organization.

1. Manpower Considerations

There is a shortage of black managerial talent in our society.[48] In many instances, blacks who have been trained for and have had experiences in other areas find themselves charged with the responsibilities of management. These individuals, in choosing their areas of educational specialization, were influenced by the limited career opportunities open to them at the time. Consequently, the choices were made in the traditional areas of professional black employment—medicine, dentistry, law, religion, education, and so forth. After varying periods of time as practitioners in the areas of their educational specialization, they have moved into management positions, either in the organizations with which they have been affiliated or in some other organization. The reasons for their assuming management roles vary—for example, their upward mobility within an organization may have been such that the next step was into management, they may have been asked to fill suddenly created voids in management because no one else with equal experience in the organization was available, they may have been offered managerial positions in recognition of their contributions and accomplishments in other areas of activity, or they may have been given these positions to effect better racial or ethnic balances in the management personnel of organizations. In many cases, the new black manager brings to the job little more than an undoubted and proven intelligence, a desire to perform well in his new capacity, the ability to get along well with people, and a high degree of adaptability. He is almost completely devoid of the increasingly technical qualifications for efficient management.

Moreover, the flow of young blacks into management is small. Several factors appear to be causally related to an apparent disinclination toward managerial careers. First, black youth share with white youth negative attitudes toward establishment institutions, whether these institutions be business organizations, labor unions, government agencies, or other not-for-profit institutions. These youth are suspicious of organizational bigness, power, and motives. They perceive basic conflicts between the objectives of establishment institutions and the solutions to the social and economic and racial problems of society. They see too few opportunities for personal involvement with the solution to these problems because they are convinced that these institutions are not only unconcerned about the problems but that the realization of organizational objectives actually increases and intensifies the problems. Second, there are too many token black managers and not enough genuine managers to serve as models for the aspirations of black youth. In the corporate world, where many blacks have gone directly after graduation—ostensibly into management positions or into jobs which were supposed to lead to management position—disillusionment has followed upon what is perceived to be blind-alley jobs or discrimination in advancement opportunities; this disillusionment is communicated back to the campuses from which these students have come. Regarding government, black youth have specific additional reservations, born of experiences and relationships with government at all levels—experiences and relationships that have undermined their faith in government as an institution to which they can beneficially and realistically relate. They view the relatively few blacks who have managerial positions as token appointments in response to pressure, with the position-holders having little or no decision-making power or authority. These perceptions tend to be reinforced by what these youth regard as indifference—if not hostility—on the part of government toward the socioeconomic problems of blacks. Third, many black graduates come from colleges which, because of a shortage of financial and other resources and/or because of adherence to traditional liberal-arts concepts, as noted earlier, do not provide the type of undergraduate backgrounds necessary for success in graduate management study programs. Fourth, opportunities for management education and careers for qualified blacks simply are not known on the campuses of most of the colleges where these students are obtaining their undergraduate education. Coupled with this lack of knowledge is a lack of understanding of the nature and scope of management on these campuses, and confusion between management as a socially useful function and as a money-grabbing, socially-aggressive economic activity.

Thus, there is the need both to increase the managerial capabilities of existing black managers and to increase the supply of these managers, in the interest of sound and sustained black economic development. Many graduate schools of management–business–business administration have attempted, and are attempting, to address the problem of the shortage of black managers by providing financial or other assistance for black students to pursue graduate study in management. The Consortium and the Council on Graduate Management Education (COGME), as well as the number of independent universities outside these two groups, are examples of the assistance which has been made available. It is clear, however, that programs offering fellowship aid and remedial training to black students—while valuable—represent only a short-term solution to the problem of increasing the supply of black managers. A long-term solution is also required. Such a solution would involve enlarging the flow of interested students coming out of predominantly or traditionally black colleges, establishing programs to make certain these students are better prepared for entry into graduate programs, and developing ways to make them more positively oriented toward the opportunities a career in management would offer; in short, what is needed is a program designed to go upstream of current efforts to make sure that potential black managers are able to take advantage of the fellowships and other educational opportunities available to them.

2. Organizational Considerations

The planning and implementation necessary to move from a less desirable economic situation to a more desirable one must be systematized and coordinated. This, in turn, presupposes some type of organizational structure with well-defined echelons of responsibility and authority. To some extent, these organizations already exist at local levels in the form of community development corporations. The number of these corporations should be greatly increased, to cover both urban and rural areas, and they must have the resources —financial, human, and otherwise—necessary to be effective instruments of change with respect to local black economic development. Wherever possible, cooperative arrangements between these corporations and local black institutions—i.e., colleges, churches, fraternal orders, fraternities, sororities, business groups, trade and professional organizations— should be effected. Wherever possible, also, the local corporations should effect maximum cooperation with predominantly white institutions—colleges and universities, chambers of commerce, trade associations—which are interested in and can be of assistance to the black economic development effort. In such cases, however, it should be clearly understood that the corporations have the ultimate authority and responsibility.

The local community development corporations should be organized into regional groups—Northeast, Middle Atlantic, Southeast, Southwest, Midwest, and West. The regional organizations would facilitate uniformity of approach and methodology, to the extent that local conditions permit, and they would be clearinghouses of information on black economic development policies, programs, and problems for their respective regions. The most important function of the regional organizations, however, would be providing links between the local corporations and the national organization concerned with black economic development.

The federal government must become more meaningfully involved in the process of black economic development —in planning, in the allocation of resources, and in the implementation of programs and projects. More meaningful involvement under the current system—with programs and responsibilities scattered over several departments and literally scores of agencies—is practically impossible. It is increasingly clear that the extremely complex nature of black economic development necessitates a coordination of effort at the national level. This can best be achieved by having all programs and responsibilities lodged in a single agency. Since this agency must, of necessity, interface with other agencies, it must have a stature which the other agencies will respect. It is therefore suggested that a new department be added to the cabinet. Since black economic development must be related to the economic development of other racial and ethnic minorities in the country, it is further suggested that the new department be named the Department of Minority Economic Development. Since blacks account for approximately 95 percent of the nonwhite or minority population of the country, its secretary would be black. Key positions in the department, below the level of secretary, would be staffed by members of other minority groups more or less in accordance with their proportions in the total nonwhite or minority population. Further, since economic development requires an interdisciplinary approach, it is also suggested that the secretary of the department be provided a group of advisors made up of representatives of organized minority professionals in the several disciplines—e.g., the Caucus of Black Economists, the Black Caucus of the American Sociological Association, the National Conference of Black Political Scientists, and so forth. Representatives of these organized minority professional groups should also make their services available at the local and regional levels to the maximum extent possible.

SUMMARY

Black economic development must occur within the context of, and will be constrained by, conditions and trends of the national economy. Subject to these limitations, there is much that can be done to improve the economic situation for blacks. It is essential that the process for this improvement be characterized by planning, which includes the establishment of goals, the choice of the best means of achieving these goals, the most efficient allocation of resources to action programs, and the direction and coordination of program implementation.

The major goals of black economic development are closing the black-white gaps in the indicators of economic well-being, a more equitable distribution of income within the black community, and increased upward mobility of black people. In order to achieve these goals, the quality of the black labor force must be improved, including a greater diversity of marketable skills; a more effective utilization of black manpower must be realized; there must be greater assurances of decent standards of living in the absence of ability to earn income; increased consumer education is essential; and the accumulation of wealth must be greatly increased.

The management of black economic development will necessitate a great supply and increased quality of black managers. Equally important is an organizational structure which includes economic development corporations at the local level, regional groupings of these corporations, and a Department of Minority Economic Development within the cabinet of the federal government. This new department would better assure the necessary government commitment to and involvement in black and other minority economic development.

Chapter Five

Black Business Development

Black business has been described as a "social myth," created during the last decade of the nineteenth century as a means for blacks to achieve equality within a "system of separation and subordination," institutionalized by the founding of the National Negro Business League by Booker T. Washington and associates in Boston in 1900, and propagated by repeated exhortations "to spread the faith in salvation by business" and by repetitions of success stories of individual black businessmen.[1] This conclusion—the result of analyses by a brilliant black sociologist, E. Franklin Frazier, in *Black Bourgeoisie*—has engendered much controversy among blacks (and, probably, some whites) as to the past and present realities of black business enterprise as well as its prospects for the future. The description is fairly current, since it is contained in a book published in 1957, and the author died in 1962. Apparently, Frazier saw no reas to change his mind before his death. During the latter part of the 190s—and especially as a consequence of the assassination of Dr. Martn Luther King, Jr., in 1968—some fundamental changes began to occur with respect to the institution of black business enterprise. These changes, however, were not sufficient to impress yet another eminent black scholar, Andrew F. Brimmer, this time an economist and governor of the Federal Reserve Board, who, after examining the economic evidence, expressed considerable doubt about the contributions of and prospects for black business.[2]

This chapter analyzes the past and current situation of black business, and suggests some directions and changes which are necessary if it is to become a truly viable instrument for black economic development in the years to come.

THE HISTORY OF BLACK BUSINESS ENTERPRISE[3]

Business enterprise is not a recent black phenomenon. Long before they were forcibly uprooted from their African cultures and brought to the Americas, blacks prospered as merchants and traders in Africa and other societies offering them freedom of movement. For example, the powerful rulers of Ghana, Mali, and Songhay—the three great black kingdoms of West Africa, that flourished during the period of the Dark Ages in Europe—traded throughout North Africa as well as in parts of Europe and Asia. During the sixteenth century, viable and prosperous business activities—based largely on specialized skills such as weaving, pottery, woodworking, and metallurgy—continued despite the decline of the West African kingdoms and the subsequent resurgence of tribalism.

The forced separation of blacks from their natural environment, the ruthless destruction of centuries-old black cultures, and peculiar and degrading socioeconomic arrangements which characterized the black man's beginnings in America combined to undermine the heritage of black business enterprise that the first American blacks brought with them to this continent. Moreover, severe limitations on black economic activity, which were consistent with the constitutionally imbedded concept that blacks were something less than human beings and, therefore, not entitled to the basic rights of human beings,[4] accompanied their transformation from merchants to merchandise.

Prior to the Civil War, black business ventures were confined largely to small-scale, personal-service types of enterprises, operating within the framework of well-established and rigidly enforced patterns of prescribed behavior. Because slavery was an integral part of each colony's system, and because laissez-faire England had empowered each colony to deal with the slave problem as it saw fit, slave codes were enacted in each of the colonies which effectively circumscribed the economic activity of black slaves. For example, in about 1700, the New York Colonial Council enacted a law providing that "no servant or slave shall give, sell or truck any commodity whatsoever during the term of his service," which was followed by a 1707 statute rendering all bargains or contracts with slaves null and void and preventing all trading with any slave without the owner's consent.[5] A New York City regulation of that time prevented slaves and servants from selling "large quantities of boiled corn, peaches, pears, apples, and other kinds of fruit."[6]

In spite of their improved political status, black freedmen found their business activities circumscribed nearly to the same extent as when they were slaves. Their activities in the South were limited to those in which whites did not want to engage or services they did not want to perform for blacks. In the North, racial oppression, keen competition from white entrepreneurs, the success of immigrants in displacing blacks, and a relatively sparse and greatly dispersed black population were the major limitations on black business. Successful black business enterprises consequently tended to be those that catered to the most personal needs of black people. Enterprise was to a considerable extent associated with the birth, existence, beautification, and burials of other blacks.

Examples of black businesses that flourished despite the constraints imposed prior to the Civil War date back at least to 1736, when a former slave, Gabriel Bernoon of Providence, Rhode Island, opened a catering service, the first ale and oyster house in that city. Perhaps the most outstanding of the pre-Civil War black business owners was Paul Cuffe who, in 1780, at the age of twenty-one, began his own shipbuilding and sailmaking operation. By 1806, this Bostonian had a fleet of one large ship, two brigs, and several small vessels, and had begun financing several Back-to-Africa expeditions. Other notably successful black entrepreneurs during the period were Robert Allen and James Forten of Philadelphia. Allen manufactured boots and shoes, founded the African Methodist Episcopal Church, and together with Absalom Jones cofounded the Free African Society of Philadelphia, which operated a mutual aid society that was the first black insurance organization in this country. James Forten was a prosperous sail manufacturer. In addition, Henry Boyd (a manufacturer of bedstands and other types of furniture in Cincinnati), William Alexander Leidesdorff (a California shipping tycoon), and Barney Ford of Denver (hotel and restaurant owner), were prominent businessmen before the Civil War.

In the years following Reconstruction, as noted earlier, economic activity was stressed as a means of solving the "race problem." Although the Emancipation Proclamation, coupled with this emphasis on entrepreneurship, improved the environment for black ownership and operation of business enterprises, the number of black businesses did not increase appreciably until 1885. Two factors coincided with this increase—the increasing urbanization of blacks; and the black community became increasingly dependent on black business, and vice versa, as white support for both declined. Thus, while the year 1890 found 31,000 blacks engaged in business, the number in 1900 had increased by 30 percent to 40,000.[7] The majority of these enterprises were concentrated in areas related to skills developed during slavery (e.g., barbering, restaurant-keeping, catering, gardening, retail-food marketing, milling, brick-masonry, painting, blacksmithing, building, etc.). Moreover, they tended to be very small. For example, in 1899, a study was conducted by W. E. B. Dubois of black enterprises with $500 or more of capitalization; the enterprises covered totaled 1906.[8] During the period, however, some enterprises which could hardly be classified as small for that time, were established. These included the various enterprises of Frank and Dow Reed, in Macon County, Alabama; the catering enterprises of John J. Trower of Philadelphia, and William E. Gross, Peter Van Dyke, and Thomas Downing, and Francis J. Moultry of New York; the hotel operations of E. C. Berry of Athens, Ohio, and Joseph W. Lee of Squantum (a suburb of Boston); the undertaking enterprises of Elijah Cook of Montgomery and James C. Thomas of New York; the street railway and other enterprises of Wiley Jones in Pine Bluff, Arkansas; the various enterprises of John McKee in Philadelphia, Thomas Lafon, in New Orleans, and of Dr. A. D. Redmond in Jackson, Mississippi; the grocery store of Victor H. Tulane in Montgomery; the bookstore of Granville Carter in Greenville, Mississippi; and the bakery business of H. K. Rischer in Jackson, Mississippi.[9] Other significant enterprises established during the period included the Coleman Cotton and Woolen Mills in Concord, North Carolina, the Mount Alton Mining and Land Company of Virginia, Wormley's Hotel of Washington, D.C., and a substantial truck gardening firm in Charleston, South Carolina. Other businesses created at that time which are still in existence include the North Carolina Mutual Life Insurance Company, Atlanta Life Insurance Company, Overton Hygienic Products Company, Madame Walker's Poro System, the National Baptist Publishing Board, and the Afro-American Newspaper.[10]

Banking was not ignored by these early black owners and operators of business enterprises. In 1888, there was not a single black bank in the United States. In 1908, twenty years later, fifty-five black banks had been started, and forty-seven were in operation—eleven in Mississippi, ten in Virginia, five in Oklahoma, four in Georgia, four in Tennessee, four in North Carolina, four in Texas, two in Alabama, and one each in Arkansas, Pennsylvania, and Illinois. The oldest of these banks—and "the best established Negro bank in the United States" at the time[12]—was the savings bank of the Grand Fountain of the United Order of the True Reformers in Charlotte County, Virginia, which opened for business on April 3, 1889, as the result of a charter granted by the Virginia legislature in March 1888. The origin of this bank is significant in that many of the black banks in existence in 1908 were started through the efforts of black fraternal orders—the oldest of which, the Masonic order, was established by Prince Hall on March 6, 1775.[13] These fraternal orders were the most important mobilizers of black finance. The black church, which was the second most important agency, in this respect, was the moving force behind the establishment of most of the other black banks.

The golden era of black business development occurred during the 1920s, which spawned more black-owned enterprises than any other decade before or since, raising the total estimated number of black-owned business enterprises to 80,000 by the time of the 1929 stock market crash. The unprecedented growth of black businesses during the twenties stemmed mainly from the expansion and assistance of black-owned banks, which made loans available on terms unobtainable either from the white banking community or from other capital markets. The stock market crash and the ensuing depression unfortunately closed not only the doors of many black businesses, but also those of thirteen black banks that had provided much of the financial backing for the business expansion of the 1920s.

Black business ownership revived during the early and middle thirties, increasing to an estimated 103,870, but then declined to 87,475 by 1940. Whereas the earlier increases were attributable to "buy black" and "support your own" campaigns, the subsequent decreases underscored the incapability of these campaigns to maintain the operations of the more marginal enterprises.

The World War II economy, the federal government's policy of extending equality of opportunity by granting subcontracts to black enterprises, and assistance to veterans in establishing business enterprises were all causative factors in the prosperity of black businesses in the 1940s. During the next two decades, however, these enterprises began increasingly to experience unforeseen, but logically predictable, difficulties. Many of these enterprises had prospered in a limited black economy behind the protective walls of segregation. With the civil rights successes in desegregating public accommodations, many black-owned service and entertainment-oriented enterprises were unable to compete with the better established white-owned similar enterprises.

THE CURRENT STATUS OF BLACK BUSINESS

As mentioned earlier, according to official statistics, there were 163,000 black-owned business firms in the United States in 1969—or about 387,000 less than the 550,000 enterprises that blacks would have owned if their ownership equaled the officially estimated proportion of blacks in the total population. The 163,000 firms amounted to 2.2 percent of all business firms and to 50.6 percent of all minority-owned business firms in the country that year. Business receipts of the black-owned firms amounted to $4.5 billion—0.3 percent of all business receipts, and almost 42.5 percent of all minority-owned business receipts.

The numbers of firms (in thousands) and the business receipts (in billions of dollars) for 1969, for blacks and other minority groups, by broad industry categories were as follows:[14]

TABLE 18

Black and Other Nonwhite Business Ownership in 1969

Industry	Number of Firms Owned		Business Receipts	
	Blacks	Other Nonwhites	Blacks	Other Nonwhites
Contract construction	16	14	$0.5	$0.5
Manufactures	3	5	0.3	0.4
Transportation and other public utilities	17	7	0.2	0.2
Wholesale trade	1	4	0.4	0.6
Retail trade	45	51	1.9	3.3
Finance, insurance and real estate	8	14	0.3	0.2
Selected services	56	45	0.7	0.8
Other	17	19	0.2	0.3
Totals	163	159	$4.5	$6.2

The above data show that with a larger number of firms than other nonwhites, blacks had the same or a smaller volume of business receipts in contract construction, transportation and public utilities, and selected srvices. If the ten most important groups of black-owned enterprises are ranked in order of total business receits (in millions of dollars) as compared with these same enterprises owned by other nonwhites, and if an average per enterprie is calculated for each group, a better comparison of the competitiveness of black v. other nonwhite enterprises is possible.[15] (See Table 19). Thus, among the ten most important groups of black enterprises, blacks appeared to fare considerably better in the case of wholesale trade, and only slightly better in car dealerships, service stations and retail stores, than do other minorities. In all other categories, the other nonwhites showed better performances. Taking the group of enterprises as a whole, however, it should be noted that the other nonwhites did only slightly better on the average than did the blacks—i.e., per enterprise receipts of $56,391 v. $56,006.

TABLE 19
Competitive Position of Black Businesses in 1969

Industry Group	Black-Owned		Owned by Other Nonwhites		Average Receipt per Firm (dollars)	
	Receipts	Firms	Receipts	Firms	Blacks	Other Nonwhite
Car dealers & service stations	631	6,380	550	5,706	98,903	96,389
Food stores	438	11,268	1,055	11,224	38,871	93,995
Wholesale trade	385	1,660	553	3,819	231,928	144,802
Eating & drinking places	360	14,125	593	13,193	25,487	44,948
Personal services	288	33,906	244	19,346	8,494	12,612
Special trade contractors	284	13,477	265	9,413	21,074	28,153
Retail stores	278	6,412	306	7,115	43,356	43,008
General building contractors	140	2,359	142	1,805	59,347	78,670
Trucking and warehousing	134	7,252	95	3,736	18,478	25,428
Real estate	78	5,524	144	7,616	14,120	18,907
Total, as % of all enterprises	67.4%	62.8%	64.0%	52.1%	—	—

The data show that black businesses tend to be concentrated in the personal services and retail trade areas. The Small Business Administration estimated in 1969 that 20.8 percent of all black businesses were oriented toward personal services (as compared with 5.5 percent of white-owned businesses) and that 27.7 percent of black-owned businesses were in the retail trade (as compared with 27.2 percent of white businesses).[16] Only 13.6 percent of all black-owned businesses provided nonpersonal services, compared with 18.5 percent for white-owned businesses. In addition, 10 percent of all black enterprises were in the construction industry, 1.8 percent were in manufacturing, and 26.1 percent in other miscellaneous types of business. The comparable figures for white business were 11.5, 5.5, and 31.8 percent.

Even though personal services and retail trade enterprises predominate black entrepreneurship, blacks are underrepresented in even those businesses. For example, black ownership accounted for only 8.2 percent of all personal service enterprises, and for only 2.2 percent of all retail trade outlets. For other types of business, black-owned enterprises accounted for 1.9 percent of all construction firms, 1.6 percent of all nonpersonal services firms, 0.8 percent of all manufacturing facilities, and 1.8 percent of all other types of enterprises. In view of the estimated $47 billion spent by blacks in the United States during 1970, the incongruity of these statistics is particularly glaring.

The impact of black business on the national economy is negligible—and, as important as they may be economically, socially, and psychologically to the black owners, their importance to the total black economy is only slightly less negligible. For example, the black-owned business receipts of $4.5 billion were less than 10 percent of total gross sales to blacks.

An analysis conducted by this writer of black entrepreneurs in seven urban areas—Atlanta, Cleveland, Durham, Jackson, Los Angeles, Norfolk, and Richmond—revealed characteristics which may be considered fairly representative of black enterprises in general. The average annual gross income of these enterprises was $29,895; the average net profit was $6454; and full-time and part-time employment averaged 3.75 persons per enterprise.[17] The analysis confirmed the findings of other studies—i.e., the concentration of business in retail and personal-services enterprises, the majority were sole proprietorships, many of the owners had full-time or part-time jobs outside the enterprise, the majority of the owners had less than a high school education, and most of the entrepreneurs were over forty years old.

The current relative insignificance of black business enterprise largely results from a number of obstacles within the black businessman's external environment. That the mitigation of these obstacles can lead to viable and vigorous black businesses is being proved by the emergence and apparent successes of a new type of black businessman in recent years. These businessmen are taking advantage of some of the more basic economic and technical opportunities; they are establishing enterprises that are providing needed goods and services to the total public and not just to the black community; they appreciate the fact that there is not one set of principles and prerequisites for white-owned enterprises and another set for those owned by blacks; and they are aware of such considerations as capital requirements, market potential, labor availabilities, and the technological state of the arts. The list of businesses owned and operated by these entrepreneurs, although they currently account for only a fraction of the total black businesses, is long and varied—and becoming increasingly so, on both counts.[18] What is needed are sound programs for overcoming the obstacles to moving more black business into the economic mainstream and providing the means whereby black business can make its proper contribution to black economic development. It is to this task that the remainder of this chapter is directed.

IMPROVING AND EXPANDING BLACK BUSINESS ENTERPRISE

Dun and Bradstreet has recorded and analyzed commercial and industrial business failures in the United States for more than 100 years. In an analysis of 13,514 reported business failures in 1965,[19] Dun and Bradstreet found that inadequate experience and general incompetence accounted for 92.5 percent of all manufacturing failures, 89.3 percent of all wholesaling failures, 91.3 percent of all retailing failures, 92.9 percent of all construction enterprise failures, 91.6 percent of all failures among commercial service firms, and 92.4 percent of the combined total of all business failures. According to Dun and Bradstreet's figures for 1965, the business failures caused by inadequate experience and general incompetence are attributable in varying degrees to the following factors: inadequate sales (40.7 percent); competitive weakness (21.0 percent); heavy operating expenses (13.3 percent); receivables difficulties (9.0 percent); inventory difficulties (5.1 percent); excessive fixed assets (4.1 percent); poor location (3.6 percent); and miscellaneous (3.2 percent).

Although Dun and Bradstreet's figures do not specifically include a record of black business failures, black businessmen often make the same mistakes as their white counterparts. They are, however, plagued by an additional set of unique problems, which are visited upon them solely because they are black. For example, Eugene Foley, a former SBA administrator and director of the Economic Development Administration, includes the following in a list of factors restraining black business development:[20] dependence upon a predominantly black trade; natural racial antipathies exacerbated by socioeconomic conflicts; a lack of both business success symbols and a business tradition, which stems largely from inequalities of past opportunities; the paucity and weakness of black ethnic institutions—except perhaps for the black church—with a resulting lack of political strength and unity; and white racism, as manifested by segregation and the economic relationships between the black ghetto and white society.

The thrust of programs designed to bring black entrepreneurs into the mainstream of this country's free enterprise system must be directed toward overcoming the unique problems the black businessman faces. A multiplicity of programs ostensibly directed toward this objective exists (or has existed) within both the public and private sectors, many with dubious results because of inadequacies of funding and/or interest. Several departments and agencies at the federal level were empowered to organize programs specifically designed to encourage and assist black and other minority business development. The more important of these programs include the Technical Assistance and other programs of the Economic Development Administration, wihch provide technical assistance to business enterprises in disadvantaged areas;[21] programs of the Office of Minority Business Enterprise (coordination of federal activities dealing with the problems of minority entrepreneurs, mobilization of the private sector to assist minority businessmen, stimulation of the minority community, and dissemination of information important to minority business development);[22] the Manpower Development and Training Program (institutional), administered by the Department of Health, Education and Welfare;[23] the Model Cities programs, which provided for funding for the development of businesses in target urban areas receiving grants from the Department of Housing and Urban Development for the purpose of addressing the problem of urban blight on a demonstration basis;[24] relocation payments to businesses displaced by federal highway development, urban renewal, and other federal projects;[25] urban renewal demonstration programs; Federal Housing Administration insured loans for the construction and rehabilitation of housing for low- and moderate-income families; the construction and leasing program of public housing units, administered by the Department of Housing and Urban Development; and the Special Impact programs of the Office of Economic Opportunity.[26] The Special Impact programs are designed to solve problems of "dependency, chronic unemployment, and rising community tensions" in areas with large concentrations of low-income persons. The statute specifically states that the programs should, "where feasible, promote the development of entrepreneurial and management skills and the ownership or participation in ownership of assisted businesses by residents of the area served." Under Special Impact, OEO has given a number of grants for equity capital and administrative expenses to community development corporations (CDCs) to establish their own businesses. Special Impact grants have also gone to venture capital pools, administered by community organizations, for business development in the target area.

In addition to the above, other federally financed programs include the Service Corps of Retired Executives (SCORE), which provides management assistance to small businesses being assisted by the Small Business Administration (SBA), with emphasis on encouraging small business entrepreneurship among minority groups;[27] the guarantee-leasing program for the space needs of small commercial and industrial enterprises;[28] the Local Development Company program, which provides long-term loans to local development companies or private entities that receive SBA funds to assist small business in acquiring land, in constructing, converting or expanding buildings, and in purchasing machinery and equipment;[29] and the Minority Enterprise Small Business Investment Company (MESBIC) program, under which SBA makes long-term loans to privately owned, for-profit companies which, in turn, make long-term equity or debt investments in small minority business enterprises;[30] Operation Business Mainstream, which is a package program that coordinates the efforts of SBA for maximum results in delivering financing and services to disadvantaged businesses;[31] the "8(a) set-aside" program, under which the SBA provides a form of sheltered government market, through its subcontracting program under the Small Business Act of 1958, to businesses in low-income areas, even when their bids on government procurements are not competitive;[32] regular business loans, by which the SBA seeks to assist all enterprises coming within the broad definition of "small businesses";[33] and economic opportunity loans, which provided funding for businesses in low-income areas on more lenient terms than the regular business loans of SBA.[34] Other SBA programs have included government-backed franchising operations, and the "6x6" Pilot Loan and Management Program.

Two major problems exist with respect to each of these and every other federal government program as well. First, blacks are often unaware that such programs exist. Secondly, local and state officials of the federal departments and agencies administering the programs often exhibit negative attitudes toward blacks who seek assistance. These criticisms apply as well to the myriad state and local government programs, many of which promise to conform to federal equal-opportunity guidelines in order to obtain federal funds but later ignore their promises and the federal guidelines once funds are obtained. These factors undoubtedly relate to the fact that in Tennessee, for example, in the year ending June 30, 1973, a total of 329 loans amounting to $19,647,000 were made; of these totals, thirty-five loans amounting to $690,000 went to minority businesses. For the period July 1, 1973–April 30, 1974, in Tennessee, 157 loans for $12,096,000 were made, of which fourteen loans amounting to $483,000 went to minority businesses.[35] For the entire nation, in fiscal year 1974, through May 31, a total of 24,821 loans amounting to $1,762.6 million were made, of which 6081 loans for a total of $251.1 million went to minority businesses.[36]

Coincident with the violent urban eruptions involving over 200,000 persons, causing nearly 8000 injuries and 191 deaths between 1964 and 1970, was a "commitment" by the private sector to seek solutions to the problem of under-representation of blacks and other ethnic minorities in business ownership and control. The "awakening" of the private sector was not, however, limited to minority entrepreneurship. It purported to encompass employment, housing, welfare, education, and the general voicelessness and powerlessness of blacks and other minorities, as well as business. Within the context of this chapter, however, an illustrative list of programs would include those of: the Interracial Council for Business Opportunity; the Chase Manhattan Capital Corporation; the Arcata Investment Company; the program for corporate purchases from minority firms under the sponsorship of the National Minority Purchasing Council; the Cleveland-based Black Economic Union, formerly the Negro Industrial and Economic Union; the Opportunity

Funding Corporation; the Minority Contractors' Assistance Program; the National Alliance of Businessmen; the American Institute of Certified Public Accountants; the Progress Association for Economic Development; the International Council of Shopping Centers; the Ford Foundation; the Menswear Retailers of America; and various essentially local programs in urban areas across the country.

The assistance provided by these and other programs designed to encourage the expansion and improvement of black business enterprise has borne fruit. As examples, of the top 100 black enterprises listed in *Black Enterprise, June 1974*, the following have been among those receiving public or private assistance during the past decade or so: Watts Manufacturing Corporation of Lynwood, California (metal products manufacturing); All-Pro Enterprises, Inc., of Pittsburgh (fast-food franchising); Progress Aerospace Enterprises, Inc., of Philadelphia (subsystem manufacturing); Fighton, Inc., of Rochester, New York (electrical equipment and metal products manufacturing); Northtown Big Star of Nashville, Tennessee (supermarket); Vanguard Volkswagen of Pagedale, Missouri (automobile dealership); Garland Foods, Inc., of Dallas, Texas (meat processing); TAW International Leasing, Inc., of New York City (equipment leasing); Myers Century Chevrolet, Inc., of Upper Darby, Pennsylvania (automobile dealership); Blatche's Foods, Inc., of Hartford, Connecticut (supermarket); Renmuth, Inc., of Detroit, Michigan (metal fabrication); The Kenwood Co., Inc., of New York City (furniture, liquor retailing, and real estate management); and others. The owners and managers of these enterprises have demonstrated beyond any doubt that, if given the opportunities long denied, blacks can be successful in business—and that that success does not have to be dependent upon maintaining the walls of racial segregation.

Assistance for black business development began in 1900, with the formation of the National Negro Business League, now known as the National Business League (NBL), mentioned earlier. The NBL today has local chapters in more than seventy urban areas throughout the country, and its membership is a highly diversified segment of the black business community. Using funds obtained from the Office of Economic Opportunity, the Economic Development Administration, the Small Business Administration, and the Office of Minority Business Enterprise, the NBL during the past several years has provided a comprehensive package of financial and technical services to black enterprises in Atlanta, Atlantic City, Chicago, Cleveland, Columbus, Durham, Houston, Indianapolis, Jackson, Jersey City, Memphis, Milwaukee, Norfolk, Oakland, Richmond, Seattle, and other cities.

During the 72nd Annual Convention in Dallas, October 3–6, 1972, the NBL membership agreed upon a redirection of effort that may prove to be significant for black business development. The New Thrust, as the redirection is called, essentially seeks to accommodate the aspirations of all groups organized either to promote the business lives of their geographic areas or to eliminate the economic isolation of their constituents. Thus the NBL's new direction is toward becoming a federation of minority business and trade associations. Pursuant to its New Thrust, the NBL has undertaken a reorganization that will make an expanded package of services available to its individual and associational membership. The new services will include training and education research, and assistance in dealing with government agencies. Some progress pursuant to the redirection is discernible, but it is yet too soon to make a definite evaluation. If the New Thrust is successful, the NBL will have come full circle, because it was out of the NBL that the numerous other black business and trade associations were originally formed.

These programs—both public and private—have been of assistance, but much more will be required if a truly vibrant black business community is to evolve. Improvements in three major areas are necessary for the realization of this objective—i.e., increased alertness to business opportunities, improved technical and managerial capabilities, and greater financial availabilities.

1. Alertness to Business Opportunities

An examination of the statistics on the country's gross national product (GNP) for the years 1950–1972 reveals a generally upward trend in the importance of services produced—from 30.5 percent of GNP in 1950 to 41.9 percent in 1972, with a value of $482.3 billion in 1972. In constant 1958 dollars, these services—including electric, gas and sanitary services, wholesale and retail trade, finance, insurance, real estate, services of government and government enterprises, medical care, transportation, education and research, religious and welfare activities, and personal services—increased in value by more than 122 percent (to a total of $392.7 billion) between 1950 and 1971.[37] There is no reason to suspect that service-oriented production will not continue to be increasingly important in our economy. This shift of production in the economy provides overall guidelines as to current and predictable opportunities for black enterprise development.

Big business enterprises provide opportunities for black business expansion and improvement which have been only minimally exploited. To cite only a few examples, (a) the Partners-In-Trade program of twenty-five large U.S. corporations, all experienced in foreign trade, which is designed to assist small enterprises in starting or expanding in the export trade;[38] (b) the programs for licensing of business opportunities of corporations, by which these large firms provide technical data and consultations, development studies, and other services for operations based on the commercialization of live patents still held by these corporations;[39] (c) many large companies often conduct training courses for their own personnel, on subjects of immense value to existing and prospective small business owners and managers, to which these small business owners and managers are welcome; (d) the National Minority Purchasing Council, a program specifically for minority business enterprises by which the top-level management of large firms set goals of purchasing from minority enterprises while providing services designed to effect a better identification and utilization of minority suppliers of products and services needed by larger firms;[40] (e) the Patent Surveillance Service of the Manufacturers' Institute (of Oxford, Michigan) which provides information, for a nominal charge, on patent-licensing opportunities and on new profit opportunities arising from the expiration of patents; and (f) franchising opportunities with reputable firms in a diversity of areas, including both products and services.[41]

In addition to the opportunities for black business to engage in export trade, under the Partners-In-Trade program mentioned above, the possibilities for conducting business abroad appear to be good. The less-developed countries of Africa and in the Caribbean seem to offer the best opportunities, but the more highly developed countries of Europe should not be ignored. The most successful model is probably cooperative or joint ventures with nationals of the foreign country, but the establishment of an enterprise owned solely by American blacks cannot be ruled out in the case of every country. In cooperative or joint ventures, American blacks, in some instances, must be prepared to take minority positions and to conform to other regulations. These other regulations may include, but are not necessarily limited to, the number of host-country nationals that must be employed and in what capacities, legal and tax consequences of various relationships to the U.S. company (e.g., branch, subsidiary, base company, etc.), and legal procedures for establishing enterprises and conducting business in the host country.

Opportunities for domestic joint business ventures with established white enterprises—aside from the licensing arrangement described above—and with white individuals should not be overlooked by existing and potential black entrepreneurs. Entirely aside from possible technical and managerial expertise and financial resources made available to black entrepreneurs—both to be discussed in the succeeding subsections—such joint ventures could (not necessarily would) provide (a) ready access to essential trade and business information not normally available to black business men and women; (b) another perspective in decision-making processes; (c) complementarity and supplementation to the black entrepreneur's capability in the day-to-day operations of the business; (d) a stronger organizational structure for the enterprise; and, perhaps most important, (e) ease of entry into two markets (i.e., the minority black market and the larger market of the total society). The possible advantages of black-white enterprises must, of course, be compared with whatever disadvantages there may be. No general statement is possible, other than that these opportunities should not be ignored, and each opportunity must be analyzed on its own merits and prospects.

In the transition of areas from white to black or racially mixed neighborhoods, opportunities exist for blacks to acquire some established retail and other enterprises currently owned by whites. A major advantage in acquiring such enterprises is usually the fact that they are on-going businesses with established customers and sources of supplies. The decision to acquire an established business, however, should be made only after satisfactory answers to a series of important questions have been obtained. For example, one needs to know prior to purchase (a) why the current owner(s) wishes to sell the business; (b) what has been the history of the business, what is its present condition, and how do the past and the present relate to future expectations; (c) the nature and extent of management necessary for successful operation; (d) the relationship between the selling price and the current value of the enterprise (based on such evaluation methods as forecasted sales, anticipated return on investment, capitalization of future earnings, value of inventory, value of supplies, and/or property assets and accumulated depreciation); (e) the certifiability of the enterprise's past and current financial statements; (f) financing terms the current owner(s) will be willing to accept, and what will be the source(s) from which additional funding beyond a down payment can be obtained; (g) how and when the transfer of ownership is to be effected, the nature of relationships (if any) after ownership has been transferred, and other contractual matters; and (h) how valid is the evidence of ownership possessed by the seller. Assuming answers to these questions are satisfactory, the prospective new black owner may wish to consider retaining the former white owner, as an employee or consultant, until he becomes thoroughly familiar with the enterprise.

Acquiring established enterprises in racially changing neighborhoods should not be the extent of efforts of blacks to acquire ownership in or control of white enterprises, however. From time to time—for reasons ranging from profitability to social consciousness—white owners of business enterprises provide opportunities for blacks to purchase all or parts of these enterprises. Whereas taking advantage of these opportunities may be impossible for individual blacks, it would be possible for blacks combined as a group for the purpose, or for existing black religious, fraternal, and other organizations. In taking advantage of these opportunities, prior consideration should be given to the list of questions suggested just above.

Finally, opportunities appear to exist for black entrepreneurship in finance and insurance, in which there are practically no black-owned and black-controlled businesses to date. These include (a) consumer financing (the volume of which was $32 billion in 1972); and (b) property and liability insurance (the premiums written on which amounted to about $36 billion in 1971). Entry into these highly lucrative fields, of course, will require detailed preorganization feasibility and other studies as well as the mobilization of considerable financial resources.

2. Technical and Managerial Capability

Many current and potential black business owners and managers have the technical competence necessary for the type of business in which they are interested or involved, gained through long employment in the field or otherwise. The more serious deficiency—often more serious than the lack of adequate financial resources—is the managerial competence.

To the extent that improvements in technical capability in a particular type of business are necessary, however, several forms of assistance are readily available. Some of these have already been suggested—i.e., technical assistance made possible through patent licensing agreements with larger corporations, franchising arrangements, joint ventures, and retaining the former owner of a business as an employee or consultant. In addition to these, technical assistance is available from several volunteer trade associations and professional groups. For example, under the Ownership Opportunities Program, cooperation is provided between a manufacturer, the trade association, and a retailer in the operation of retail menswear enterprises.[42] Other groups that have indicated their willingness to provide technical assistance to black business owners include accountants, attorneys, engineers, marketing specialists, public relations experts, and shopping-center specialists. Of increasing importance, also, are the colleges and universities, many of which include in their regular curricula many technical courses which are of great assistance to business owners and managers; some of these institutions will often put on special courses just for the business community, and will make available faculty and students for the specific purpose of assisting small- and medium-sized business and enterprises.

The demarcation line between technical and managerial capabilities and functions is not always clear in a small business, because the owner-manager usually must shoulder both responsibilities. It is for this reason that the management of a small business is often more difficult than managing a large one. It should be clear that, generically, management means the planning, budgeting, organizing, directing, and controlling of productive resources in a maximally efficient manner—and that, with respect to the management of a business enterprise, the measure of maximum efficiency is maximum profits. Herein lies one of the major problems of many black-owned and black-managed business enterprises —i.e., the belief that as long as a business is returning a profit, it is doing well. This belief may be deficient in at least two ways: the profit may not be a profit at all in a strict accounting sense; and if it is a true profit, it may not be as great as it might be with more effective and efficient management.

Management is not an innate characteristic of the individual. Despite the "gut feeling" about how to manage a business—and some have this to a greater extent than others —effective and efficient management results from the acquisition of certain knowledge and skills. In addition to the management process itself (as defined just above), and entirely aside from the knowledge of basic business principles, the successful management of a business enterprise requires knowledge and skills in the areas of problem-solving, analyzing, and adjusting to the external environment, organizational structure and development, relationships with employees and customers, decision-making, and financial management. These are all areas of crucial importance, but special emphasis on financial management is warranted.

Financial management is often the determinant of success or failure of business, regardless of the racial or ethnic identification of the owner or manager. Financial management requires a knowledge of, and familiarity with, financial planning and budgeting, including long-range forecasting methodology; evaluative analysis of allocative methods and cost elements; cost-benefit analysis; financial ratios (i.e., liquidity, leverage, activity, and profitability ratios); financial control, including especially break-even analysis; cash-flow analysis; and the development and utilization of performance evaluation criteria.

A most effective manner of acquiring necessary management knowledge and skills is by an organized system of learning situations, involving lectures, seminars, workshops, simulation and other teaching–learning methodologies. This usually means a course in an organized setting over a protracted period of time, and many black businessmen and women can afford neither the time nor the cost of such a course. It is possible, however, to acquire the knowledge and skills at little or no cost, and with a minimum of interference with the running of the enterprise. For example, in the fall of 1972, forty-seven colleges and universities began cooperating with SBA in a new management–assistance program called the Small Business Institute; by fall 1973, the number of colleges and universities had grown to more than a hundred, and the number increased even more during the 1973–1974 academic year. Under the program, each college or university contracts with SBA to provide management assistance to eligible business enterprises—eligibility being based on financial assistance from SBA either in the form of a direct loan or an SBA-guaranteed private loan. Counseling to the business enterprises is provided by students (preferably seniors) enrolled in a degree program in business administration.[43] Other management assistance is available for the existing or prospective black businessman, including the programs of colleges and universities not affiliated with SBA in the above program, the Interracial Council for Business Opportunity, Progress Association for Economic Development, and others. (A listing of government and private organizations with programs designed to assist black business appears in Appendices B and C.)

A recent development could be of extreme importance

in improving the managerial capabilities of black businessmen and women. The National Task Force on Education and Training for Minority Business Enterprise, headed by Dr. Robert M. Worthington of Rutgers University (formerly associate commissioner in the Office of Education), made its report with action proposals after studies extended over a period of eighteen months. The importance attached to the charge of the Task Force is indicated by the fact that the Department of Labor and the Department of Health, Education, and Welfare cooperated with the Office of Minority Business Enterprise (OMBE) in the conduct of the study, by the fact that the Task Force is a unit of the Interagency Council for Minority Business Enterprise (composed of representatives of every federal department and agency involved in the development and promotion of minority enterprise), and by the fact that it was seen fit to appoint seventy-three individuals to the Task Force. The proposals contained in the report included the establishment of forty local delivery systems to provide basic management training by June 30, 1974; increased support for fellowships, scholarships, and loans for formal business training for minority students; increased support to predominantly black colleges to improve and expand undergraduate and graduate business management programs; joint effort by OMBE, the Office of Education, and SBA, in cooperation with selected institutions of higher education, in the establishment of a two-year associate degree program for small business ownership; cooperative efforts between the federal government and private industry in increasing apprenticeship, internship, and similar opportunities for potential minority business owners; and a program designed to develop awareness of business as a career and provide some business training for minority youth, including those at the elementary and secondary educational levels.[44] If the proposals of this Task Force are effectively and efficiently implemented—i.e., if the necessary manpower and financial resources are made available to implement the proposals—the results could be beneficial in both the short and long run.

3. Financial Resources

The most publicized hindrance to black business development is the inability to acquire adequate financing. In many instances this is due to racial discrimination, but the imposition of standard objective criteria by lending institutions in making a decision with respect to a loan would often dictate a negative response to the prospective loan applicant in the absence of racial discrimination. For example, in many instances, the applicant does not have much of a track record in the business for which he is seeking financing, the planning and financial documentation to support the application is often unsatisfactory—or inadequacies or inconsistencies in statements about financial requirements may exist. There can be no doubt, however, about the need for greater financial availabilities if black business development is to proceed —and there also can be no doubt about the limitations imposed heretofore by racial discrimination.

The National Advisory Council on Minority Enterprise —created on March 5, 1969, by Executive Order 11458— clearly recognized the need for more positive action in this area. In its final report, submitted in the fall of 1970, the Council made the following pertinent recommendations: (a) an increase in minority-group ownership of, and community participation in, savings and loan associations, commercial banks, and other financial institutions; (b) officers of federal and state governmental agencies, such as the Federal Home Loan Bank Board, to be urged to increase the number of new financial institutions which are organized, managed, and controlled by minority-group Americans; (c) the increased use of purchasing power by the public and private sectors to assist existing minority enterprises and to encourage the establishment of viable new business enterprises; (d) the achievement as a matter of major national priority substantially increased minority ownership of economic resources in both urban and rural areas; (e) the reintroduction and enactment of lease-guarantee and performance-bond assistance; and (f) the commitment of $930 million in federal funds—over the fiscal years 1972, 1973, and 1974—to foster and upgrade 6000 businesses annually with an average capitalization of $110,000 (with $60 million of this amount to be made available to local-level delivery system organizations; $40 million for experimental and demonstration projects; $500 million to be used for leveraging additional funding of a magnitude of three and one-half to four times that amount by—for example—using standard SBA guarantee treasury deposits, $170 million to go for management and technical assistance, and $160 million to be utilized for business and management education.)[45]

Implementing the recommendations of the Advisory Council means assigning a fairly high priority to minority business development as a national objective. In point of fact, the Advisory Council, in its final report to President Nixon, also stated that "high on the list of priorities for the decade of the seventies is the provision of a substantially increased stake in the American economy for members of minority groups. This will come about through expanded opportunities for ownership of economic resources. Enormous economic inequities, the product of centuries of disregard, discrimination, and institutional racism still exist, although the public and private sectors have moved to curtail active discrimination and the exclusion of minorities from economic opportunity. A major, long-term commitment of resources, energy, and imagination is required if America is to remedy this centuries-old injustice."[46]

As a national objective, minority enterprise development, presumably, would be beyond the pale of partisan politics. This would obviate the necessity for each new administration to formulate its own program. The fact that each new administration has, in fact, formulated its own program for minority-enterprise development has created a feeling within the minority communities that they are recurringly in the position of having to start all over again whenever there is a change in national administration in Washington. Thus, not only have the faith and confidence of blacks and other minorities in the American economic system been challenged, but its political superstructure makes assistance to minority business more expensive than would otherwise be true. National objectives which transcend partisan politics are not unusual in this country; entirely aside from considerations of national defense and security, and space exploration, the list of precedents includes agricultural subsidies, various types of assistance to oil exploration and exploitation, and a long list of other special interest programs. In this instance, the special interest group would consist of almost one-fifth of the country's total population, all minorities included.

The current administration in Washington is certainly aware of the problem, and on several occasions statements have been made which appeared to reflect an awareness also of the need to assign a high national priority to minority business development. As examples, entirely aside from being generally credited with coining the words "Black Capitalism" during his 1968 presidential campaign and his promise "to get the people of the ghetto into private enterprise," President Nixon has (a) pointed out "the need for capital and the recognition of the special financial problems small businesses may face in their early years,"[47] and (b) observed that "Both morally and economically, we will not realize the full potential of our nation until neither race nor nationality is any longer an obstacle to full participation in the American marketplace," and that "expansion of business opportunities was one of the most effective means now available for advancing the cause of human dignity among minority Americans."[48] Moreover, as noted above, he created the Office of Minority Business Enterprise, the National Advisory Council on Minority Enterprise, and the National Task

Force on Education and Training for Minority Business Enterprise.

The prestigious Council and Task Force have completed their studies and made their recommendations or proposals. OMBE has been in existence long enough for all to be cognizant of the deficiencies inherent in its sub-Cabinet status. Effective action—as opposed to more rhetoric, more studies, and more experiments—is now the order of the day. The creation of the Department of Minority Economic Development suggested in the preceding chapter, with an assistant secretary for Minority Business Development, is the next logical step in giving substance to promises and recreating minority faith in the American free-enterprise economic system and in its political superstructure.

The implications of such federal leadership for the private sector could be tremendous. Encouraged by such leadership, there might be several institutions across the country like the Chase Manhattan Capital Corporation providing assistance for minority-owned enterprises such as (a) long-term equity financing, (b) the subordination of assistance provided to loans from banks or insurance companies, (c) arranging bank financing, (d) the development of new markets and the expansion of existing ones, (e) counseling services by independent consultants, (f) consultation on future capital needs, (g) the location of managerial talent, (h) arrangements for merger discussions and acquisitions, and (i) a concentration on the financing of new and small business enterprises for the economically disadvantaged in the ghetto and other depressed urban areas.

Encouraged by such leadership, the immense resources of nonbanking financial institutions, which amounted to $603.6 billion at the end of 1967,[49] might be made available in greater volumes for the financing of black and other minority business development and expansion. Of these institutions, some of the life insurance companies have made available $2 billion primarily for black business development, although financing for multifamily housing was also included in the total. The resources of the other institutions have hardly been tapped.

Encouraged by such leadership, the joint government-private sector campaign to increase funds deposited in minority-owned banks might have been far more successful than raising the total from $400 million in 1970 to the recently reported "over $1 billion."[50] Instead of 500 companies responding to the drive, there might have been twice that many and the 500 might have been induced to deposit even more than they did. State and local government agencies as well as agencies of the federal government might have swelled the deposits from this sector many times over. With the addition of such deposits, the minority banks could become more than social ornaments—they could become real instruments for minority business and economic development.

SUMMARY

Foreseen after the Civil War as the means of securing equality for American blacks in a racially hostile and discriminatory society, black business enterprise has not fulfilled that promise. Despite this failure, there have been notable examples of individual black business successes dating back before the Revolutionary War and continuing to the present.

Limitations imposed by white America as to the types of economic activity open to blacks effectively directed black business ventures mainly into areas in which whites did not want to engage and/or into providing essential personal services for other blacks. The formidable barrier of racial segregation provided the basis for success for many of these ventures. With the social and political successes of the civil rights struggle following World War II, however, many of these enterprises were unable to compete with better established white enterprises which began to offer goods and services in exchange for the black American dollars. Thus, about 1968, a new and different type of black business enterprise began to emerge—one more in step with economic and technological changes in our society, patterned more among lines of white enterprise, and competing with these enterprises for the patronage of the entire society.

Although these new enterprises are making their mark, their impact on both the black community and the total society is as yet almost negligible. It seems clear that if the black business community is to become truly viable, and if it is to make its proper contribution to black economic development, more enterprises based on fundamental characteristics and trends in the total economy—as well as a continuation of traditional black businesses—are necessary. For both the old and new types of black businesses, increased technical, managerial, and/or financial capabilities are required.

The need for increased capabilities in these three areas is widely recognized, and specific recommendations by reputable national groups have been made for increasing their availabilities to existing and potential black business owners and managers. What is lacking is a national will for successful black (and other minority) business development. If the resolution is great enough, in terms of needed resources devoted to the task, it will happen. That drive—that resolution—will continue to be lacking, however, in the absence of top federal government leadership. The Department of Minority Economic Development could be the motivating and guiding force for black and other minority business development, assuming the provision of resources necessary to accomplish the task.

Chapter Six

Prospects and New Approach

Thus far, the black economy has been analyzed and progress has been noted. Also brought out were the serious gaps between the state of economic development of the black community and that of the majority of Americans. Some suggestions have been made for closing these gaps and thus improving the economic quality of life for black Americans. Two fundamental questions now emerge. First, can the changes necessary for black economic development occur in a system in which the productive apparatus is privately owned—but only minimally by blacks—and in which the major decisions are motivated primarily by profit considerations? Second, is contemporary economic development theory applicable to the special problems of the black subgroup within American society? On the basis of answers to these questions, an approach to black economic development is suggested.

BLACK ECONOMIC DEVELOPMENT WITHIN THE SYSTEM

Opinion is rather sharply divided on whether black economic development, on the scale necessary for black Americans to participate equitably in the economic life of the United States, is realizable within the existing economic structure and its sociopolitical superstructure. An objective analysis of prevailing economic concepts, relationships, and parameters, it appears, could provide the basis for broader agreement.

1. The Name of the Game

The economy of the United States has undergone changes which have moved it progressively farther away from its nineteenth-century approximation to the model of pure capitalism. Despite the changes, characteristics of the pure model persist. Perhaps the strongest of these characteristics is the system of motivation which guides economic decision-making with respect to the allocation of resources, incentives for production, and reactions to changing economic conditions. This motivational system is market-oriented with particular emphasis on profit-seeking, if indeed not profit maximization.[1]

The pursuit of profits dictates actions which may (and often do) penalize blacks (and other disadvantaged groups). According to economic theory, the maximum profit position of a firm—whether under conditions of perfect or imperfect competition—is when marginal revenue and marginal cost are equated. If a firm cuts production before that point is reached, it is denying itself more in revenue than it would have to pay out in costs; if it goes beyond that point, it is incurring more in costs than it is receiving in revenue. For example, see table on p. 135. When production increases from 10 units to 11 units, the total cost of production increases from $15 to $20; the marginal cost of the 11th unit, therefore, is $5. Similarly, the marginal cost of production for the 12th unit is $6, or the difference between $20 and $26. On the revenue side, when the quantity sold increases from 10 units to 11 units, there is an increase in total revenue from $20 to $25, or a marginal revenue of $5; when the 12th unit is sold, the total revenue increases from $25 to $29, or a marginal revenue of $4. The illustration also shows that the point of maximum profit for this hypothetical firm is when it produces and sells 11 units, or where the marginal cost and marginal revenue are each equal to $5; if the firm produces beyond this point, it adds $6 to total cost but only receives $4 in additional revenue, and if it stops before that point (given the trend of the marginal cost and marginal revenue figures), it would have given up in revenue something more than $5 and would have paid out in cost something less than $5.

Quantity Produced	Total Cost	Marginal Cost	Quantity Sold	Total Revenue	Marginal Revenue
10	$15	–	10	$20	–
11	20	5	11	25	5
12	26	6	12	29	4

To proceed with the likely effect on blacks (and other disadvantaged groups) of the pursuit of maximum profits, attention is directed to the concept of marginal cost. To simplify matters, it is assumed that the only cost of production which the hypothetical firm above has is the cost of labor. It is further assumed, in the interest of simplicity, that the firm can always buy labor at the same wage per unit. Under these assumptions, the only reason for the marginal cost to increase is that the marginal product of the last worker hired is less than that of the worker hired just before him—i.e., diminishing productivity returns. Thus, marginal cost and productivity returns are opposite sides of the same relationship—if one goes up, the other goes down, and vice versa.

Because of deficiencies in educational and employment opportunities, largely the result of past and present racial discrimination, the marginal productivity of blacks tends to be lower and the marginal cost consequently higher than in the case of whites. The employer of labor, if he is interested in maximizing profits, will hire the higher-productivity and lower-cost white, even in the absence of racial discrimination. The black worker, under these conditions, would only be hired if the price of the goods produced for sale increases to the point that marginal revenue will cover his marginal cost. If hired and the price of the goods decreases, the higher-cost and lower-productivity worker—in this instance, the black worker—will be the first to be laid off. This will, of course, be recognized by the reader as the familiar last-hired-first-fired dilemma which characterizes black employment.

2. Corporate America and Black Economic Development

In recent years, and especially since the black rebellions of the mid-1960s, there appears to be a development or deepening of social consciousness on the part of many corporations. Programs to assist the black hard-core unemployed in becoming working members of society have been developed, plants and other employment providing enterprises have been located in the ghetto, major corporations have assisted in the establishment of small black manufacturing affiliates to make component parts for their products, franchising opportunities have been extended to blacks, and other noteworthy efforts have gotten underway.

During recent years, some of the leading corporations have elected blacks to their boards of directors. At the end of 1973, reportedly, approximately eighty-five blacks have been named to such positions. The corporations include some of the giants—General Motors, Chrysler, Ford, American Telephone and Telegraph, International Business Machines, Lockheed, Metropolitan Life Insurance, Prudential Insurance, Twentieth-Century Fox, and Westinghouse.[2] Presumably, this means that these corporations would, seemingly, be more responsive to the problems and aspirations of the black community. If so, this will undoubtedly have beneficial effects for black economic development.

Moreover, many leaders in corporate America have opened formerly closed employment opportunities for blacks in managerial and technical positions. This also contributes to overall black economic development, in the sense of both higher incomes and increased employment/career opportunities. A list of these corporations includes those who have placed blacks on their boards of directors plus others. These include Exxon, Bendix, World Book Encyclopedia, Procter & Gamble, Quaker Oats, Sony, McGraw-Hill, Xerox, and Houghton Mifflin.[3]

Despite these undeniable contributions, some of the basic needs in the black community have not been addressed. Black economic development depends upon these needs being met. Many of these needs are collective needs—quality education, adequate transportation, recreational facilities, sanitation services, housing, in a word, livable inner-cities. Providing these services does not constitute profitable ventures, and thus private enterprise does not perceive of providing them as part of its responsibility. It thus becomes the responsibility of government—local, state and federal—to make the services available. But providing the services requires the allocation of productive resources for the purpose. In our economic system, the allocation of resources is the consequence of the "dollar-votes" of consumers in the marketplace operating through the mechanism of derived demands. Since productive resources are scarce—i.e., if they are allocated for one purpose they are not available for other purposes—it is in the interest of the corporate sector that these resources be allocated in a way that is designed to produce profits. To ensure the proper allocation of productive resources, corporate enterprise (l) spends vast amounts of money in advertising identical products under different brand names in order to develop consumer preferences, in adding useless frills and decorations to commodities in order to attract new customers and retain old ones, in incorporating early obsolescence into products so as to assure quick repurchases, and in manipulating consumers into becoming aware of wants and needs of which they were previously ignorant (all expenditures, of course, being recouped by charging prices higher for goods sold to consumers than would otherwise be necessary), and (2) brings to bear on government its collective power, in the form of lobbies or otherwise, to prevent government from mobilizing resources to provide the needed social, public, or collective services.

In the pursuit of its own selfish goals, of course, corporate enterprise clothes its arguments in the guise of defending the free competitive enterprise system. Defense of the system—which is presumed to be one of the major causes of the country's phenomenal overall growth and development—is akin to defense of the American flag. The defense chooses to ignore or obscure the fact that the free-enterprise system of the United States has been gradually but steadily supplanted by a persistent trend toward monopoly capitalism. For example, in 1970, there were 1,655,000 active corporations in existence in the country.[4] Nine and nine-tenths percent of these corporations had business receipts amounting to 85.5 percent of all corporate receipts ($1.5 billion out of $1.7 billion);[5] corporations with assets of $250 million and above (i.e., 1200 corporations, or 0.1 percent of the total number of corporations) accounted for 58.1 percent of all corporate assets ($1.5 billion out of $2.6 billion);[6] the largest 100 industrial corporations had 62.3 percent of the $463.9 billion in sales of all industrial corporations, and these corporations accounted for 38.8 percent of the assets of the largest 500 industrial corporations;[7] the largest ten retailing corporations accounted for 53.6 percent of the $73.6 billion in total sales by all retailing corporations, and these ten corporations had assets amounting to 57.7 percent of the assets of the fifty largest retailing corporations;[8] and the 100 largest manufacturing corporations held 48.5 percent of the total assets of all manufacturing corporations and 60.4 percent of the assets of the 200 largest manufacturing corporations.[9] That the trend toward increased concentration is continuing is attested to by the fact that, in 1972, the assets of the 100 largest industrial corporations had increased from 38.8 percent to 45.9 percent, with sales increasing slightly from 62.3 percent to 62.4 percent.

The concentration of economic power carries with it ever increasing and already tremendous political power, which further assures the dominance of profit making over meeting collective needs. If an example is necessary, the extremely powerful influence of the automobile industry and those industries associated with it—the oil, iron and steel, rubber, glass, road-construction, and insurance industries—in support of highway development legislation and in opposition to rapid-transit development should suffice. Both these transportation developments are intimately related to the economic well-being of blacks'—highway development, because it usually means the displacement of black homes, businesses and churches; rapid-transit development, because it could facilitate blacks, being able to commute from the jobless areas in which they are forced to live to outlying areas which provide employment opportunities.

The domination of government by giant corporations, while dictating neglect of collective needs, does offer some opportunities for black (and other minority) business development. These opportunities have been created by the military-industrial complex which has become such a very significant and, apparently, very permanent sector within our economy and society. When it becomes necessary for government to allocate resources and embark on expenditures for defense, corporate opposition—which is loud and financed with huge amounts of funds in the case of social needs—is strangely quiet. There are at least two reasons for this quietude. The first is that many of the corporations have expanded into multinational—and even international—corporate status. A strong domestic military posture, under the circumstances, is necessary to protect their far-flung empires. The other reason is that corporate America profits immensely from huge defense expenditures. For example, (1) of the top twenty-five of *Fortune Magazine's* directory of the 500 largest corporations, only five were not among the 100 largest contractors for the Department of Defense in fiscal year 1968—and one of those five was the largest contractor for the Atomic Energy Commission,[10] and (2) military-related employment accounted for 68 percent of all manufacturing employment in 1967.[11] The opportunities for black business development lie in the provision of goods and services to these corporate giants which it would be uneconomic for them to provide for themselves. Some black business enterprises are prospering by providing these goods and services, and efforts to expand this type of business should be encouraged. A moot issue emerges, however—i.e., do the benefits derived by the black businesses, which are essential to black economic development, offset the neglect of black collective needs, the fulfillment of which is also essential for black economic development?

3. The Size of Black Business Units

The vast majority of black business enterprises are small —and, as compared to the corporations discussed above, very small indeed—as measured by any standard usually employed to distinguish small enterprises from medium or large ones. As such, costs per unit of product or service tend to be high, because the enterprises seldom achieve a size which makes possible lower production or operating costs as a result of economies of scale. These enterprises begin, and remain, small because of one or a combination of three factors. These are (a) limited access to or availability of financial resources, (b) limited markets, and (c) the law of scale. The access to or availability of financial resources was discussed in the previous chapter.

In the case of a significant percent of black enterprises, the nature of the business is the provision of local services of one kind or another. The markets for such business do not expand greatly. Another reason for the smallness of many black businesses is that they cater primarily—in some instances, completely—to the black community. Taken as a whole, the black market in the United States is conservatively estimated as representing annual sales in the magnitude of $30–$60 billion. It is, however, a market which is widely dispersed and, except for a relatively few types of enterprises (e.g., insurance, cosmetics. magazine publishing, some food products, etc.), it is not economically feasible to attempt to market commodities or services beyond a restricted radius of the location of the enterprise. Other limiting factors include unfamiliarity with and inability to conduct research in distant markets, costs and other constraints on producing for and selling in extended markets, increased complexities introduced by the necessity of utilizing longer distribution channels, and the highly competitive nature of retailing (i.e., the type of business in which most black enterprises are concentrated).

The basic reasons underlying the causal factors resulting in limited markets for black enterprises are fairly obvious. For the most part, these reasons tend to fall into one or the other of two categories. First, the historical limitation on the types of businesses which society has deemed to be legitimate for blacks has dictated a concentration in enterprises which provide not only a local service but a local service for the black community. Second, until fairly recently, blacks were denied the type of education, training, and experience which would lead to knowledge and expertise necessary in coping with extended markets.

The law of scale is one of the embodiments of the law of production—the other being the law or principle of diminishing returns. The law of scale has reference to the effect on input or cost per unit of output as the size of a plant, firm, or management unit increases. If input or cost per unit of output decreases as the size of the operation increases, the operation enjoys "economies of scale"; if the input or cost per unit of output increases with an increase in the size of operation, the result is "diseconomies of scale."[12] Economies of scale may be the consequence of both external and internal forces. If external, they are the result of advantages provided by other industries or developments outside the plant, firm, or management unit. Internal economies of scale usually involve what is termed "advance in knowledge" or "pure technical advance," and are manifested by increased productivity flowing from the development of new concepts and their utilization in the productive process.

In the case of internal economies of scale, the basic causal factor is the increasing efficiencies in the utilization of productive resources as the size of the operation increases. These increasing efficiencies may, for example, flow from increased specialization and division of labor, the substitution of machinery for labor, or the introduction of a new production technique. To use an example, equipment depreciation charges and the implicit cost of a farmer's own labor, per unit of production, are likely to be lower on a farm of 100 acres than on a farm of ten acres. Whether or not the per unit costs are lower on the larger farm will depend upon the farmer's ability to manage the larger farm. And, this is the heart of the matter of economies of scale—i.e., they derive largely from the ability to manage increasing quantities and varieties of productive resources (i.e., workers, machines, land, and raw materials or semifinished goods).

The limited managerial capabilities of most black business owner-managers place a definite limit on the quantities and varieties of productive resources they can effectively and efficiently coordinate. Beyond a certain point—usually somewhere between *small*–small and *large*–small—diseconomies of scale are experienced as more and more varied productive resources are added to the enterprise. An important consequence of this limitation on the quantities and varieties of productive resources that can be managed is the fact that black enterprises are, for the most part, forced to concentrate in activities in which economic and feasible operations dictate relatively small-sized enterprises. This tends to exclude blacks from most manufacturing. Limited managerial capabilities, however, have adverse consequences even in black enterprises where economic and feasible operations coincide with relatively small-sized enterprises. The result is that seldom do black enterprises expand in size sufficiently to benefit from economies of scale (e.g., the use of mechanized equipment, the ability to put to use advanced techniques, and advantages accruing from specialization and division of labor).

Again, characteristics of the environment determined for blacks provide reasons for inadequate and, in terms of business operations in our economy, largely irrelevant capabilities. Employment and career opportunities outside the traditional black professions—i.e., education, medicine, dentistry, law, mortuary science, and theology—were extremely few until very recently. Thus, there was a pronounced scarcity of models for black youth to emulate in fields other than the traditional ones. Under the circumstance, it is understandable that black education—and this was the only type of education available to black youth until only a very few years ago—did not include preparation for a life of work other than in those fields in which employment was certain.

4. Upward Black Mobility

The denial of equal opportunities to minorities and their rejection as a group, by society as a whole, according to one thesis, tend to propel them toward activities geared to ensure economic security. The case of the Jews in many countries during the Diaspora, the Chinese in Southeast Asia, the

Indians in East Africa, the Lebanese in West Africa, and different immigrant groups in the United States, for example, often are used as references for the documentation of this thesis. The example of immigrant groups in the United States, who have broken out of their ghettos and carved lofty economic niches for themselves in our society, is often used in attempts to prove the basic inferior "somethingness" of American blacks. The question often asked is some variation of "If poor immigrants, many of whom could not even speak English, can come to the United States and achieve economic successes within a generation or so, why cannot blacks who have been here for centuries do the same?" There are several reasons for the invalidity of the analogy.

First, the idea of black inferiority, initially conceived and endorsed by the U.S. Constitution as a justification for slavery, has been the rationale for a systematic debasement of blacks throughout the postslavery period. This debasement, designed to keep blacks "in their place," has taken various forms. These include unreasoned violence against blacks when they have sought to exercise the rights of citizenship, legalized racial segregation, the most complete economic oppression and exploitation, and many other deterrents to upward mobility for blacks.

Second, members of the white majority benefit from the existence of a depressed minority. For example, white workers are protected in their higher-paying jobs from black competition by racial discrimination in employment and advancement, by planned imperfections in the blacks' knowledge of the labor market, and by the racially exclusionary practices of many labor unions. Middle-class and upper-class whites are assured of a source of supply of cheap domestic labor. White owners—as well as some blacks and other nonwhite owners—of ghetto real estate reap enormous profits from black tenants by overcrowding, overcharging, and neglecting maintenance. Ghetto merchants grow fat on the sales of shoddy merchandise at exorbitant prices on usurious credit terms. White employers benefit both by the lower wages they pay to blacks, and by the existence of this cheap labor supply also used as a threat to keep their white employees in line.

Third, as a result of past and present denials of educational and training opportunities, blacks are becoming increasingly unemployable as a consequence of rapid technological improvements. This is manifested in the fact that, during the past fifteen or more years, the black unemployment rate has been consistently about twice the unemployment rate of whites.

Fourth, the immigrants with which the critics are wont to compare blacks are white. Thus, they are more easily assimilated into the majority society. Often, this assimilation may require—or the immigrant or his offspring may perceive the requirement—a change of name or the spelling of a name. This, of course, is much more easily effected than changing the color of one's skin.

THE INAPPLICABILITY OF CURRENT DEVELOPMENT THEORY

The black economy has many characteristics in common with those of contemporary under-developed countries. This has caused many social scientists to view the black economy as an under-developed country. The consequence of this analogy or identification has been suggestions for development policies and programs, based on concepts and utilizing the tools of one or another existing economic development theory, patterned after those applied in the under-developed countries. The problem often encountered is that much of contemporary development theory is based on the experiences of industrialized countries, and these simply don't apply to under-developed country situations, unless some fairly basic modifications are made.

Contemporary development theory, it seems, is even

less applicable to the black economy of the United States than it is to under-developed countries. For example, Kenneth Boulding has observed, "When we look at the economics of race, the individualistic bias of economic theory leads to an insensitivity to the problems of identity, especially group identity, which are so prominent now. We are going through an agonizing struggle to find the proper place of racial groups within the integrative structure."[13] Thomas Palm notes that "Although the procedures of modern economies on both the theoretical and applied levels have provided important insights into interracial relationships, there are three major limitations to the usefulness of established doctrines."[14] The limitations perceived by Palm are (1) the assumptions about the human behavior of middle-class whites which constitute the basis of the "usual generalizations about economic propositions," (2) the assumption in existing theory that the "patterns of interpersonal relationships and the social machinery are given," and thus not subject to change, and (3) differential black status cannot be explained on the basis of either logic or data because the issue of racism transcends economics and gets into philosophical concern with esthetics, semantics, and particularly ethics.

A major reason modern development theory cannot be applied to the case of the black minority in the United States is the fact that rational economic choices, upon which so much of the theory is based, are denied to blacks. The options available to black Americans in almost every area of economic activity—and in absolutely every area of importance to black economic development—are severely circumscribed by the precepts and institutions of white racism. The type and quality of education, the uses to which labor power and productive effort may be put (as well as whether they will be utilized), and consumption patterns—now almost as in slavery—are all determined for blacks by whites. Moreover, the proscriptions on and prescriptions for black economic activity are applied, for the most part, to blacks as a group, with exceptions made for individual blacks.

The temptation to generalize, in matters of this kind, is almost irresistible. Objectivity, scientific inquiry, and basic integrity, all require bases for allegations. Thus, it becomes essential to examine the major theories of economic development in terms of their relevance to black economic development.[15]

1. The Classical Theory

The model of economic development attributed to the classical economists is as follows:[16] (a) output is a function of the size of the labor force, the amount of land or natural resources available, the stock of capital, and the level of technique (with land itself being considered fixed and discoveries of new natural resources apparently treated as a part of technological progress); (b) the level of technique depends on the level of investment (i.e., in order to take advantage of the opportunities presented by ever-present improved techniques and new commodities, new net investment—or investment over and above that necessary to replace worn-out machinery and equipment—is necessary); (c) net investment, or new additions to the capital stock, depends upon profits (i.e., the return on land and capital); (d) profits depend upon the net effect of the counteracting forces of size of the labor force and level of technique (i.e., an increase in the size of the population—and, thus, of the labor force—resulting in diminishing returns in agriculture with consequent increased labor costs and reduced profits v. increasing returns—and, thus, profits—in industry as a consequence of improved techniques); (e) the size of the labor force depends upon wages (with real wages trending towards the subsistence level, in accordance with David Ricardo's statement about the iron law of wages in his *Principles of Political Economy and Taxa-*

tion (1817); and (f) wages depend upon the level of investment (i.e., the amount of funds available to pay labor coming from savings effectively utilized by investing).

A superficial analysis of the model reveals the key role of capital accumulation, without which technological progress is impossible. But capital accumulation depends upon the returns on land, which David Ricardo interpreted as a tendency for the rate of profit to fall, and capital used in productive processes. As has been shown in previous chapters, the vast majority of productive resources which blacks have to contribute to the production of commodities and services is labor power. Thomas Robert Malthus, after carving a niche for himself in the history of economic thought by his pessimistic theory of population, observed, "A man whose only possession is his labor has, or has not, an effective demand for produce according as his labor is, or is not, in demand by those who have the disposal of produce."[17] Put differently, if the productive resources of a group consist solely or predominantly of labor, the economic activity and the degree of economic progress of the group are determined by those who see fit to use that labor and the amount of wages they are willing to pay for the use of that labor.

2. The Neo-Marxist Theories[18]

Karl Marx's preoccupation with economic development theory was mainly an interpretation of how development occurred under capitalism. A major difference between his interpretation and the classical model above is the strong emphasis which Marx placed upon the tendency for the rate of profit to fall because of conditions inherent in the capitalistic system. (This is in contrast to David Ricardo's earlier explanation of the declining tendency of the rate of profit due to decreasing soil fertility and consequent diminishing returns of land.) The means available to capitalists to counteract the decreasing tendency of the rate of profit, according to Marx, were to increase the exploitation of the working class by longer working hours, more intensive use of labor power, or reduction of wages. Although Marx did not himself develop an explicit theory of economic development, his views have constituted the basis of several such theories, including those of two contemporary American economists, Paul Baran and Paul Sweezy.

The socialist (or radical) economists have not formulated or argued for theories of economic development for a subgroup of a national society. Although they certainly have been alert to the special problems of subgroups in non-Socialist societies,[19] and have sought to arouse more awareness of and concern about these problems, they stress the need for the total society to make the transition to socialism. Because, however, suggestions have been made that this is the road that black economic development should take—as specifically opposed to one or another of the modern variations of the capitalistic model above—its major tenets are herein analyzed.

The core of socialist doctrine, briefly, is public ownership of the means of production, and the substitution of planning for prices and profits as a guide to production—at least in those areas of the economy which are decisive for the well-being of the total society and for the efficient functioning of the economic system. Presumably, there would still be some private ownership of the means of production, and individual profits would not be eliminated altogether. The line of demarcation between a public and a private economic activity, again presumably, would be determined by the decisiveness of the activity in terms of its relationship to the needs of society and to the efficient functioning of the system. There are, of course, other distinctions between socialism and the current socioeconomic system of the United States, which are more or less marked depending upon whether the distinction is being drawn between the current system and centralized, decentralized, or democratic socialism.[20] Major objectives of socialism in whatever form, however, coincide with two of the must goals of black economic development. These are a more equitable distribution of income and wealth, and a greater fulfillment of public or collective needs.

This agreement on ends does not mean that socialistic economic development of the black community, within the context of the larger predominantly nonsocialistic society, is tenable. For example, what government would own the means of production and plan economic activities in areas deemed crucial for black well-being? What would be the nature of the interface between that government and the one in Washington? What would be the nature of the relationship between that government and vested interests, with their tremendous economic and political power in the larger society? Would the resources necessary for black economic development, now largely owned by the private sector of a nonsocialist society, be turned over to a "government" with avowed ideological persuasions which are inimical to the interests of that sector? The answer to these and yet other questions would appear to negate the socialist route for black economic development—at least until such time, if ever, as socialism is adopted as a socioeconomic philosophy and system by the country as a whole. Even then, an improved economic status of blacks would not be assured, if the reports of class distinctions, noncooperation and nonparticipation, and political repressions in the Soviet Union are true.

3. The Schumpeterian Theory[21]

The economic development theory of Joseph Schumpeter—successively, finance minister of a Socialist government in Austria, professor of economics in Bonn and Tokyo, and (from 1927 until his death in 1950) professor of economics at Harvard—is being increasingly resorted to as economists grapple with the very complex problems of economic development in the less-developed countries and areas of the world.

The broad outline of Schumpeter's model is: (a) output is a function of the size of the labor force, the amount of land or natural resources available, the stock of capital, and the level of technique (as in the classical model); (b) savings depend on wages, profits, and the interest rate (i.e., savings of workers and capitalists will increase as income increases, and both will tend to save more as the interest rate rises); (c) total investment is divisible into induced investment (i.e., investments the result of increased output, income, sales, or profits) and autonomous investment (i.e., investments resulting from technological change and other long-run considerations); (d) induced investment is dependent on the level of profits and the interest rate (i.e., induced investment tends to rise with an increase in current profits and to fall with an increase in the interest rate); (e) autonomous investment is dependent on resource discovery and technological progress (i.e., innovation, as manifested by the introduction of new goods or a new quality of goods, the introduction of a new method of production, the opening up of a new market, the conquest of a new source of supply of raw materials or semi-finished goods, or the carrying out of a new organization of an industry); (f) innovation, or resource discovery and technological progress, depends on the supply of entrepreneurs (i.e., people who are capable of discerning opportunities for introducing new commodities and services or techniques of production, and who are willing to organize to produce the new economic goods or to utilize the new techniques); (g) the supply of entrepreneurs is dependent on the rate of profit and the social climate (with social climate being defined as the totality of economic and noneconomic factors in the environment in which entrepreneurs must operate); (h) the gross national product—GNP—depends upon the relationship between savings and investment, and the operation of the multiplier; (i) there is a direct relationship between wage incomes and the level of investment (i.e., both rising and falling together); and (j) the social climate is reflected by the distribution of income (i.e., any attempt to reduce profits, for example, tends to cause a deterioration in the social climate). Innovation and entrepreneurship are the key elements in

Schumpeter's theory. Thus, attention is directed to these two elements in the black community in an attempt to assess the applicability of the model to black economic development.

In the model, innovation depends on the supply of entrepreneurs, which in turn depends in part on the social climate. Schumpeter's "social climate" includes factors which are especially pertinent to the position of blacks in the United States—e.g., class structure; the nature and extent of social rewards, including profits; the conditions under which the entrepreneur must operate; the entrepreneur's access to precise information as to how the system operates; the distribution of income; legal or political impediments; reasonable chances for success in entrepreneurial ventures; and the acceptance or nonacceptance by society of people and conduct which are different. Moreover, in the Schumpeterian model, the entrepreneur must have ready access to capital financing in order to make effective his willingness to organize for the production of new goods or the utilization of new productive techniques. Much of this book has been a documentation of the limited extent to which these prerequisites for entrepreneurship exist, or are fostered, in the black community.

4. The Theory of Derived Development[22]

In contrast to the Schumpeterian theory is the theory of derived development. In an overall sense, the difference between the two is that Schumpeter's theory is more applicable to more developed situations while the derived development model is more applicable to the less-developed. Moreover, whereas Schumpeter's model places emphasis on supply, is production-oriented, and stresses individual virtues, derived development emphasizes demand, is consumption-oriented, and stresses social values. These differences are causally related to three basic elements of economic development—i.e., the generating or motive force, the nature of the development process, and the goal of development. For example, (a) the generating force in Schumpeter's theory is the entrepreneur, but in derived development, the government fulfills this role (because of either the scarcity of entrepreneurs, their limited contributions to development, or both); (b) whereas innovation is the nature of the development process in the Schumpeterian theory, in the theory of derived development, the process is characterized by "a widening of horizons aided by the pressure of need" (perhaps translatable into the more familiar term "the revolution of rising expectations"), a subjective realization of the opportunity to meet pressing needs, and the "demonstration effect" (i.e., the perception by the less-developed countries of themselves as being engaged in a very intense competition with the more-developed countries); and (c) with respect to goals, the establishment of a position of power for the entrepreneur in the Schumpeterian model is contrasted with increases in standards of living in the model of derived development.

The theory of derived development, as the term somewhat implies, is based on derivations from innovations elsewhere, as opposed to the innovating development envisaged in Schumpeter's theory. With specific reference to the less-developed countries, this means an emphasis on industrialization, increased urbanization, improved qualities of the labor force, increased demand for consumer goods with a consequent decrease in the level of savings, and an enhanced desire for higher standards of living combined with a decrease in the inclination to work as hard or as long (possibly only, of course, as a result of increased productivity). It also means an increased role for the government in economic activity because of (a) basic weaknesses of the private sector, (b) political pressures resulting from the desire for higher standards of living, (c) the need for economic and social infrastructures, the provision of which is not attractive to private enterprise because of the need for huge investments and long (if at all) pay-back periods, and (d) the greater need for organization in derived development as compared with innovating development.

The status of economic development in the black community is such that the theory is applicable, and yet it is not. For example, increases in both entrepreneurship and government intervention are necessary; innovation in the development process is required, but so also are a widening of horizons (leading, hopefully, to more innovation), a greater subjective realization of opportunities to fulfill perceived needs, and a more (and a more constructively) competitive spirit vis-à-vis the majority community; and an enhanced position of power for black entrepreneurs is essential, but so are increases in the average standard of living for black people. Thus, in terms of the economic development needs of the black community, innovating and derived development, incorporating emphasis on both production and consumption, and oriented toward the enhancement of both individual and social values, are necessary.

5. Other Theories of Development

Analyses of the polyglot of other contemporary development theories likewise reveal that they have only limited applicability to, and usefulness for, black economic development. Nor, indeed, were they meant by their authors to be so useful or applicable—as were not the four general theories discussed above. A brief examination of what this writer considers to be the more important of these other theories will, however, substantiate further the restricted appropriateness of modern development theories for black economic development. More importantly, the examination will add to a unified approach to black economic development which, perhaps, the reader has already discerned as emerging.

The Harrod and Hansen theories are concerned with the maintenance of and conditions for continued growth in industrialized capitalistic countries.[23] Both view capital accumulation as a sine qua non for continued growth. Both also stress, as important for capital accumulation, manpower (Harrod) or size of the labor force (Hansen); output per head (Harrod), which can be broken down into Hansen's supply of known resources and level of technique; and quantity (Harrod) or stock (Hansen) of capital available. In terms of black economic development, however, both theories are inapplicable. In the case of Harrod's theory, first, the interrelationship between savings, investments, and the interest rate, which he regards as significantly determining for capital accumulation in a national economy, would have very little meaning for a small section of a national economy, especially since it is being impacted more importantly by externalities. Second, although it is possible to treat net capital accumulation over some period of time as a discrete variable in the black economy, the increase in black output and the black average propensity to save are likely to be related to factors and forces more outside than inside the black community. Thus, his basic equation, $GC = s$ — where G is growth during a period of time, C is net accumulation of capital during that period, and s is the average propensity to save—would be of limited value. There are other, perhaps less significant "deficiencies" in terms of the concern of this book. Hansen's theory also has little usefulness as an approach to black economic development. Fundamental factors constituting parts of or implied in his theory are output, savings, taxes, induced investment, government investment, autonomous investment, rate of population growth, rate of resource discovery, and rate of technological progress. As in the case of Harrod's theory, it would be an impossible task to isolate the black causal and consequential elements in this array of factors.

Hans W. Singer has presented a model of economic development, drawing somewhat on the more general Harrod model, which also has limited applicability to black economic development.[24] The model, after illustrating an increase and disposition of per capita income resulting from assigning increasing productive resources to the nonagricultural sector, comes down to the equation $D = sp - r$. In the equation, D is the rate of economic development (i.e., growth of per capita income assumed to be proportionate to an increase in per capita capital), s is the rate of net savings, p is the productivity of new investment per unit of capital, and r is the annual increase of population. The problem of applicability lies in the key rate of net savings which, in turn, is a function of the income level. The level of savings within the black community, even if larger than is commonly supposed, is probably not adequate to provide the catalyst necessary to result in a desirable rate of economic development. To the extent that this is true, the productivity of new investment—unless based on external capital—and the increase in population are of academic importance only.

Walter W. Rostow's work, which can be viewed as a twentieth-century extension of the German historical school of the nineteenth century, enjoyed wide acclaim during the late 1950s and early 1960s as a model of economic development.[25] According to the theory, an economy is perceived as passing through five stages during the process of its development. These are (a) the traditional or primitive stage, (b) the transitional stage (during which the preconditions for growth are established), (c) the takeoff, (d) the drive to maturity, and (e) the stage of high mass consumption. Investment, entrepreneurship, technological progress, and institutional changes are all factors that causally relate to the progression from one stage of growth to the next. The theory has considerable value as a means of understanding some of the basic characteristics and interrelationships of an economy during various stages of growth. It, however, is being increasingly questioned both as an historical account of what happened during previous stages of growth of the more developed countries and as a model of growth for the less developed countries. With respect to black economic development, it is totally inadequate because, if one examines the total black economy, all of Rostow's stages are seen as existing simultaneously.

Finally, the Rosenstein-Rodan theory is perhaps the best known of those included in the controversy among economists about comprehensive simultaneous development in all sectors of the economy v. unbalanced development between these sectors.[26] The theory takes the side of comprehensive simultaneous development, and stresses the advantages to be derived from external economies if outside capital were injected into the economic system. If these external investments were large enough, they would overcome the inertia in the system by increasing economic activity, which would cause the demand for labor to increase with consequent increases in income. Presumably, the big push represented by the external investments would act as a primer, and, once started, the engine of the economy would continue to operate, possibly at an accelerating speed. From the point of view of black economic development, this theory has major attractions—i.e., the recognition of need for external investments, the possibility of increased employment (thus attacking the basic problem of black unemployment and underemployment), and the possibility of increased black income (which is one of the major goals of black economic development). A major reservation in terms of its applicability, however, is whether the managerial attitudes and capabilities within the black community are such as to manage efficiently the increased and necessarily varied economic activity envisaged. In terms of business units, for example, increased economic activity would entail some 400,000 new enterprises—to match the proportion of blacks in the total population—and many of these should be large or medium-sized, as measured by norms used in classifying business in the United States generally.

A SUGGESTED APPROACH TO BLACK ECONOMIC DEVELOPMENT

The theories of economic development discussed above agree on three prerequisites for economic development.

These are capital accumulation, technological progress (the realization of which is based very heavily on entrepreneurship), and improved manpower skills. Although the theories are not applicable without modifications—in some instances, modifications so fundamental as to alter altogether the nature of the theories—to black economic development, the general acceptance of these three essential elements provides a common bond between the theories and any reasonable approach to black economic development.

In Chapter Four, it will be recalled, the goals of black economic development were delineated as a closing of black-white gaps in economic indicators, a more equitable distribution of income within the black community, and increased black upward mobility. It will also be recalled that the means suggested for achieving these goals were increased wealth accumulation, expanded and improved entrepreneurship, increased quality and diversification of the labor force, more effective utilization of manpower, improved consumer knowledge, and assurances of decent living standards in the absence of earning capacity. The relationship between the first three—and perhaps, the first five—of these and the three prerequisites for economic development is obvious.

1. Capital Accumulation

The accumulation of capital is the result of either internal savings or external loans-grants. It is very unlikely that black income will increase sufficiently, in the foreseeable future, to effect savings-induced capital of the magnitude required to achieve the desired rate of economic development in the black community. Hence, there must be a net import of capital to augment black capital accumulations. The problem, then, is how to attract the capital into the black community for development purposes.

One device which could be utilized is a matching arrangement. Savings made available from the black community for economic development would be matched with a grant from the federal government in an amount which is ten times the amount of the savings. Funds attracted by the efforts of the black community from the white private sector —either in the form of grants, loans or investments—would count as "savings" of the black community for the purposes of this arrangement; thus, the current Minority Enterprise Small Business Investment Company (MESBIC) operations would be preserved. Savings attributable to a particular black subcommunity—e.g., Atlanta, Jackson, Philadelphia, Nashville, and so forth—would serve as the basis of the matching grant for that subcommunity. Contributions by the federal government under the America plan, described in Chapter Four, would count in the matching arrangement. The Department of Minority Economic Development, also proposed in Chapter Four, would administer the implementation of activities under this arrangement. To illustrate how the scheme would operate, assume in Locale A that black savings are in the amount of $1 million. Assume, further, that Locale A is able to attract $5 million from the white private sector.[27] The results would be as follows:

Black savings	$ 1,000,000
White private sector contribution	5,000,000
Sub-Total	$ 6,000,000
Federal Government contribution	60,000,000
Total	$66,000,000

Two questions will almost certainly and immediately come to the mind of the reader. These are (a) why should the white private sector want to invest in black economic activities? and (b) why should the federal government be willing to agree to the ten-to-one matching arrangement? In the opinion of the author, convincing answers can be provided to both questions.

The private white sector of the economy stands to gain

from an enhanced status of economic development in the black community. First, an increased level of income would increase black purchasing power beyond the currently estimated $30–$40 billion level; this means an even larger market for those white enterprises which would continue to enjoy a competitive advantage over potential and existing black enterprises. Second, to the extent that predominantly black enterprises materialize under joint-venture, patent-licensing, or other arrangements with white businesses, the latter are placed in a position of sharing financially in the gains from successful predominantly black enterprises. Third, and perhaps most important, the conduct of business —whether black or white—is best effected under conditions of social harmony and quietude; both of these are better assured in situations where blacks do not feel alienated and know that they have a financial stake in the continued existence of the system.

Why should the federal government be willing to match black savings on the basis of 10:1? First, black poverty and unemployment result in welfare and other expenditures of a sizable amount of tax dollars. According to data from the Office of Economic Opportunity, $18.3 billion was the total federal outlay benefiting low-income persons in 1970; in that year, 7.9 million nonwhites were in the low-income category, of which almost one-half were receiving some form of public assistance. Unless something is done to cure the basic causes of poverty and unemployment, the necessity for these expenditures will be passed down from generation to generation. Thus, as a result of larger investments now, the federal government can look forward eventually to a substantially decreased necessity for such expenditures in the future. Second, the tax base of the black community will be increased. This ultimate increase in revenue coupled with the necessity for decreased expenditures means a "double whammy" of benefits for the country. Third, the fuller participation of blacks in the economic life of the country would mean a significant increase in the gross national product (GNP). This increase in GNP would result from both a more efficient utilization of black manpower and increased specialization in production. Fourth, a significant amount of funds made available by the federal government to local and state governments under revenue-sharing is being utilized, overtly or covertly, in strengthening local and state law enforcement and the maintenance of peace and order. One of the major threats to peace and order, during the past decade or so, has been the legitimate discontent and consequent rebelliousness of blacks. With a more assured and decent standard of living, the discontent and rebellion will abate. As a consequence, larger shares of the local and state shares of revenue-sharing could be devoted to more productive activities, with resulting overall benefits to the total populations.

Of extreme importance to capital accumulation is ascertaining that the maximum amount of income earned will be saved. This has connotations for the status of consumption in a society. Chapters Three and Four dealt with consumerism in the black community. Here, it is only necessary to reiterate the essentiality of black consumer education, protection, and information programs.

2. Technological Progress

The undoubted relationship of technological progress to economic development has been noted by most, if not all, experts on economic development. Technological progress is a consequence of both innovation and the effectiveness of innovation (i.e., the advance of knowledge). The advance of knowledge, in turn, is the result of "the social environment and the socialization process."[28]

As noted throughout this book, the social environment in the United States so far as blacks are concerned is not one that is most conducive to economic development. The "minority thesis," which is supposed to explain why a minority group is goaded into innovational and entrepreneurial activities in the search for economic security, is not valid for black Americans, because of systematic denial and rejection as a fully legitimate and participating part of the total society. The denial and rejection have inhibited the nature of the identification of blacks with the larger society as well as the nature of the intercourse between blacks and that society.

Greater participation by blacks in the production and utilization of new technical information is essential for black economic development. This greater participation can be achieved in a variety of ways. In Chapter Five, for example, suggestions were made for patent-licensing, franchise, and joint-venture arrangements. These, however, would produce only limited results, because of the presence of other inhibiting factors. Aside from the black-white interpersonal relationships, these inhibiting factors include a minuscule black industrial complex and relatively little capital.

One means of overcoming these obstacles to enhanced technological progress would be the establishment of industrial parks, primarily for black and other minority groups. These parks would be located on land in close proximity to large black population centers. In addition to the black (and other minority-group) industrial sites, large established manufacturing corporations would be induced to locate branches in each park. In planning the parks, major attention would be directed toward a mix of industrial activities which would result in maximum complementarity for each park. The cost of acquiring the land and constructing basic facilities and services—including adequate transportation linkages with the population centers—would be borne by the local, state, and federal governments, since all three levels of government would benefit from the increased industrial activity. So far as the federal government is concerned, the proposed Department of Minority Economic Development would be the responsible agency. A specific responsibility of the department would be the coordination of industrial-park activities with the capital-accumulation activities discussed just above.

A major advantage of this proposal, from the point of view of technological progress, would be the encouragement it would give to joint research and development (R & D) efforts among the tenants of the parks. This would overcome the barrier of the expensiveness of such efforts if each industrial enterprise attempted to conduct its own R & D.

3. Improved Manpower Skills

Capital accumulation and measures designed to enhance technological progress would be practically meaningless in the absence of an adequate supply of well-trained black technical, professional, and managerial personnel. Some suggestions for expanding and improving the quality of black manpower were made in Chapter Four. Additional suggestions are made below.

Educational and training programs to improve black manpower knowledge and skills must have as one major objective overcoming the obstacles to achievement and motivation created by the past and present socialization of blacks. In some instances, this will mean rectifying damages to the individual stretching back to his having been born in a family and a neighborhood plagued by economic—and, more importantly, by cultural—poverty. In many more instances, however, it will mean rectifying defeatist and other negative attitudes that come from systematic and long-run societal denial and rejection. In overcoming these obstacles, the educational and training programs must be persuasive of the importance to black economic development of all types and grades of work—it must be convincing in its stress on the contributions which competent technicians, professionals and managers, alike, can make to achieving the overall objective.

Everett Hagen suggests two alternative approaches to planning an educational (and training) program for economic development which are worthy of consideration, to the extent that blacks can control the educational process for themselves.[29] These alternatives are the Fixed-Input Coefficients Approach and the Infinite-Price Elasticity-of-Demand Approach. The first approach would (a) estimate the rate of development, (b) on the basis of this estimate, determine the requirements for various types and grades of workers for periods in the future, (c) plan an educational (and training) program to meet these requirements, and (d) "plan the training of teachers so that they will be available in time to do the teaching in time to produce the needed trained (personnel)." For the purposes of black economic development—and despite Hagen's reservations about the "many possibilities of wide margins of error in this process of estimate"—this approach appears to be superior to the second approach, which would (a) assume that workers with all levels of general education will be needed and that these levels of education will result in incomes similar to those now received by persons with these levels of education, (b) determine the current levels of income corresponding to the various levels of general education, (c) "calculate the cost per student of each level of education," and (d) on the basis of cost-income comparison, "calculate the education per student that will yield the highest return." The first approach appears to be superior to the second, so far as black economic development is concerned, because (a) the existing educational system will provide the general education envisaged in the second approach, and (b) what is needed beyond this is individuals whose education and training are geared specifically to the needs of black economic development.

In the specific field of management, where the shortage of qualified black personnel is most crucial, in terms of the need for effective and efficient management of developmental programs and projects, a special education and training approach seems warranted. It is suggested that, in addition to the special preparation of managers for business and other types of organizations, a cadre of highly qualified generic managers be developed. The education and training of these managers would be such that they would be capable of moving into any type of organization—business, educational, health care, government, etc.—and, after providing the necessary guidance and assistance, move on to another organization which requires their expertise. This cadre would be employed and deployed, as necessary, by the proposed Department of Minority Economic Development.

SUMMARY

The pursuit of profits and continuing economic concentration are major characteristics of the environment in which black economic development must occur. Although they may constitute constraints on some aspects of that development, these characteristics also present opportunities for black business enterprise to become more of an active force in moving the black economy forward. The degree to which that forward progress will be realized, however, depends upon effective programs in the areas of capital accumulation, increased participation in technological progress, and the expansion and improvement of manpower skills.

Capital accumulation of the magnitude required is seen as requiring leverage arrangements, somewhat on the order of current MESBIC operations, in which the federal government will match black savings on a 10:1 basis. The establishment of industrial parks, with government-financed land acquisition, as well as essential facilities and services installations, is considered to be an important means of assuring greater participation in technological progress. The expansion and improvement of manpower skills should involve a greater concentration on the developmental needs of the black community; in this connection, it is suggested that a cadre of highly qualified generic managers be developed, to assist in the solution to managerial problems of all types of black organizations.

Appendix A

Federal Government Programs for Black Entrepreneurs

1. **Department of Agriculture**
   a) *Technical Assistance to Rural Cooperatives*—technical assistance to cooperatives serving farmers and other rural residents, including assistance to existing cooperatives and to groups interested in establishing new cooperatives. (Farmers Cooperative Service).
   b) *Economic Opportunity Loans to Cooperatives*—30-year, $4^{1}/3\%$ loans to cooperatives that furnish essential processing, purchasing or marketing services, supplies, or facilities to low-income rural families. (Farmers Home Administration).
   c) *Farm Operating Loans*—loans and technical/management assistance to eligible farm families to develop and carry on sound and successful operations. (Farmers Home Administration).
   d) *Cooperative Extension Services' Marketing Program*

—educational assistance to agricultural producers and producer groups, and to farm supply, marketing, and processing firms. (Federal Extension Service).

2. **Department of Commerce**

   a) *Business Development Program*—assistance to areas of substantial and persistent unemployment and underemployment to achieve lasting economic improvement primarily through new permanent jobs and better income for local residents. The assistance includes long-term, low-interest loans for land, building, machinery, and equipment; long-term low-interest loans to establish or expand industrial and commercial facilities in redevelopment areas; and working capital loan guarantees. (Economic Development Administration).

   b) *Public Works Program*—assistance in restoring economic health in certain designated areas, by helping to create conditions which will encourage the establishment or expansion of industrial and commercial enterprises which have the potential for providing new job opportunities. Assistance includes grants and loans to acquire and develop land and improvements for public works or public service or development facility usage, and to acquire, construct, rehabilitate, alter, expand, or improve such facilities. (Office of Public Works).

   c) *Technical Assistance*—promotion of and encouragement to the creation and expansion of minority business enterprises with special attention to providing stable jobs for hard-core unemployed and underemployed in economically distressed areas. (Economic Development Administration).

   d) *Project Enterprise*—to mobilize the capabilities of private corporations, commercial banks, and gov-

Federal Programs for Black Entrepreneurs 169

ernment to speed the development of minority business enterprise through the use of Minority Enterprise Small Business Investment Companies. (Office of Minority Business Enterprise.)
e) *OMBE*—coordination of all federal programs which can be of assistance to minority persons seeking to establish or expand businesses, encouragement of and assistance to the efforts of the private sector, state, and local governments and the coordination of these and federal efforts; and the establishment of a national clearing house for information on minority business enterprise. (Office of Minority Business Enterprise).

3. **Department of Defense**
    a) *Contracting with Labor-Surplus Area Concerns*—to encourage the placing of contracts and facilities in labor-surplus areas and to assist such areas in making the best use of their available resources; and to place contracts with labor-surplus area concerns, to the extent consistent with procurement objectives and where such contracts can be awarded at prices no higher than those obtainable from other concerns. (Small Business and Economic Utilization Policy, Office of the Assistant Secretary of Defense for I & L).
    b) *Small Business Prime Contracting*—designed to insure that a fair proportion of the total purchases and contracts for supplies and services for the government are placed with small business enterprises. (Small Business and Economic Utilization Policy, Office of the Assistant Secretary of Defense for I & L).
    c) *Subcontracting Program*—designed to enable small business concerns to be considered fairly as subcontractors and suppliers to contractors perform-

ing as prime contractors on government procurement contracts. (Small Business and Economic Utilization Policy, Assistant Secretary of Defense for I & L).

d) *Transition Program*—assistance to returning enlisted servicemen to make productive reentry into civilian life. (Transitional Manpower Programs, Assistant Secretary of Defense for M & RA).

4. **Department of Health, Education, and Welfare**

    Manpower Development and Training (Institutional)—designed to provide unemployed and underemployed persons with skills and basic education so that they may enter or reenter the job market or upgrade their skills, including minority entrepreneurs who can enroll in management training programs and/or have their employees receive training helpful to their jobs. (Division of Manpower Training and Development, U. S. Office of Education).

5. **Department of Housing and Urban Development**

    a) *Acquired Property*—to provide opportunities to contractors and real estate agents in the renovation and remodeling of property acquired by FHA due to defaults on mortgages they have insured. (Office of Assistant Commissioner for Property Disposition, Federal Housing Administration).

    b) *Financial Assistance to Nonprofit Housing Sponsors*—construction opportunities for entrepreneurs who can obtain contracts from nonprofit organizations receiving loans for the development of low-income and moderate-income housing. (Federal Housing Administration).

    c) *Home Improvement Loans*—construction opportunities for entrepreneurs who are capable of par-

ticipating in home-improvement work financed by FHA loans. (Federal Housing Administration).
d) *Low-Rent Housing Program*—construction opportunities for entrepreneurs to participate in the development of housing for low-income families by public housing agencies. (Housing Assistance Administration).
e) *Open-Space Land Program*—business opportunities for contractors in the program designed to assist communities acquire and develop land for park, recreation, conservation, scenic, or historic purposes in urban areas. (Assistant Regional Administrators of Metropolitan Development in HUD Regional Offices).
f) *Urban Beautification and Improvement*—business opportunities for contractors in the program designed to assist communities to implement programs for the beautification and improvement of publicly owned and controlled land in urban areas. (Assistant Regional Administrators of Metropolitan Development in HUD Regional Offices).
g) *Relocation Payments to Displaced Businesses*—relocation assistance and payments for business concerns displaced because of HUD-assisted programs. (Relocation Staff, Office of Community Development).
h) *Urban Renewal Demonstration*—business opportunities for contractors and businessmen providing urban renewal services in the program designed to foster projects to develop, test, and demonstrate better ways to prevent and eliminate slums and blight. (Office of Urban Technology and Research).
i) *Demolition Grants*—business opportunities for contractors capable of doing demolition work in the program designed to assist municipalities in demolishing structures that are structurally un-

sound or unfit for human habitation. (Renewal Assistance Administration).
j) *Rehabilitation Program*—business opportunities for contractors capable of participating in the program designed to assist individuals or families in repairing or improving residences in neighborhood development, urban renewal, and code enforcement areas, or areas certified by the locality to become such. (Renewal Assistance Administration).
k) *Urban Renewal*—business opportunities for contractors and businessmen providing urban renewal services in land acquisition and clearing, rehabilitation of existing structures, new building construction, and the installation of public improvements including streets and sidewalks, utilities, incidental recreational areas, flood protection, and the preservation of historic structures. (HUD Regional Offices).

6. **Department of Labor**
    a) *Job Opportunities in the Business Sector (JOBS)*—training of employees under the program established to stimulate private industry's interest in hiring and retaining the hard-core unemployed. (Regional Manpower Administrator Offices, and Office of Information, Manpower Administration).
    b) *Manpower Development and Training (MDT)*—training of employees under the program designed to provide occupational training for those unemployed and underemployed persons who cannot reasonably be expected to obtain appropriate full-time employment without training. (Local Office of the State Employment Service, or Manpower Regional or Area Office.)

Federal Programs for Black Entrepreneurs 173

7. **General Services Administration**
   a) *Construction Contracting Services*—providing minority contractors and entrepreneurs a list of repair and improvement contracts that could be reasonably handled by small construction contractors. (Business Service Center in each state).
   b) *Contracting to Provide Personal Property and Services*—providing supplies and services to the Federal Supply Service to fill the common needs of all government agencies, and to supply requirements of agencies under special agreements. (Business Service Center in each state).
   c) *Counseling on Doing Business with the Government*—a range of services, including consideration and attention to the interest and problems of small business and minority business enterprises. (Business Services Division).
   d) *Surplus Property Programs*—to make available and sell real and personal property which is surplus to the needs of the federal government. (Administrative and Financial Management).

8. **Small Business Administration**
   a) *Contracting With SBA*—a program which permits SBA to provide direct contract assistance to small business concerns owned and operated by economically and socially disadvantaged persons. (Procurement and Management Assistance).
   b) *Economic Opportunity Loans*—financial and management assistance to low-income or other disadvantaged individuals for small existing or potential businesses. (Economic Opportunity Loan Division).
   c) *Financial Assistance (Lease Guarantee)*—assistance to small businesses in obtaining space in commer-

cial or industrial locations not normally available to them for credit reasons. (Office of Lease Guarantee).

d) *Financial Assistance (Local Development Companies)*—long-term loans to local development companies for the acquisition of land, construction, conversion or expansion of buildings, and for the purchase of machinery and equipment for identifiable small businesses. (Office of Development Company Assistance).

e) *Financial Assistance (Small Business Investment Companies)*—long-term loans, equity capital, and management assistance to small businesses. (Associate Administrator for Investment).

f) *Operation Business Mainstream*—a program designed to encourage the economically and/or socially disadvantaged to become small businessmen and to expand their existing small business. (Office of Minority Business Enterprise).

g) *Procurement and Management Assistance to Small Businesses*—management and technical assistance, and government procurement, and sales assistance. (SBA Regional Offices, or Associate Administrator for Procurement and Management Assistance).

h) *Financial Assistance (Displaced Business Loans)*—long-term loans to businesses which suffer or will suffer substantial economic injury as a result of construction by or with federal funds. (Office of Business Loans, or SBA Administration Offices in each state).

i) *Financial Assistance (Regular Business Loans)*—financial assistance to start or assist small businesses unable to secure financing on reasonable terms from other sources. (Office of Business Loans).

9. Veterans Administration
    a) *Educational Assistance for Veterans*—management training for those veterans whose education or careers were interrupted by active duty after January 31, 1955. (Nearest VA Office).
    b) *Veterans Business Loans*—financing assistance to eligible veterans in the form of partial guaranty or insurance of loans made by private lenders for business purposes. (Nearest VA Office).

Appendix B

Private Programs for Black Entrepreneurs

1. *The Interracial Council for Business Opportunity (IC-BO)*—a coalition of black and white business and professional men with a varied program of assistance for minority entrepreneurs, including:
   a) *Technical and Management Skills Transfer*—whereby one-to-one counseling is provided to ICBO clients.
   b) *Educational Programs*—including seminars on a variety of topics essential to efficient business operations, and a series of workshops on specific industries.
   c) *Student Activities*—encompassing a program which operates more or less on the same principle as does the Big Brother concept.
   d) *Major Business Development Program*—including a National New Enterprise Program (in which assistance is provided to new business ventures requiring a capitalization of $100,000 or more) and a

Major Industries Program (in which assistance is provided to new businesses requiring a capitalization of $250,000 or more).

e) *Project Transfer*—involving the purchase and transfer of white-owned enterprises to black entrepreneurs.

f) *The ICBO Fund*—which guarantees up to 50% loans made by banks to minority entrepreneurs. (Offices in New York, Los Angeles, Washington (D.C.), Newark, St. Louis, New Orleans, Chicago, and other cities).

2. *The Black Economic Union (BEU)*—formerly the Negro Industrial and Economic Union (NIEU), to encourage black people to own and manage business enterprises through a combination of soft loans, technical assistance, and equity financing. (Headquartered in Cleveland, with offices in New York, Los Angeles, Washington (D.C.), and Kansas City).

3. *The Rochester (N.Y.) Business Opportunities Corporation*—created to serve as a development corporation to develop a means whereby assistance could be provided to blacks to organize business enterprises in the ghetto, including financial assistance, technical and advisory assistance, arrangement of guaranteed markets, and research and development of business opportunities.

4. *Economic Resources Corporation*—a Los Angeles-based corporation which buys and sells land, machinery, equipment and buildings; receives and makes grants; and guarantees loans made to approved borrowers by private lenders.

5. *The American Institute of Certified Public Accountants*—developing plans for a program to provide special bookkeeping and auditing assistance to new minority-owned firms, in cooperation with OMBE.

6. *The National Association of Accountants*—formulating plans, in consultation with OMBE, for a possible educational accounting program to aid minority businesses.
7. *The Hough Area Development Corporation (Cleveland)*—an economic development organization based on grass-roots contacts, fostering a combination apartment building and shopping center; a maintenance, landscaping and gardening operation; and a manufacturing concern to produce injection–molded products for the automobile industry.
8. *The Chicago Economic Development Corporation*—an off-shoot of the Chicago Small Business Development Corporation, it arranges financing from money–lenders for minority businessmen.
9. *The Inner-City Business Improvement Forum of Detroit*—to handle financial packaging for small businesses.
10. *Program for Action in Changing Times, San Francisco*—assistance includes:
    a) *An Economic Development Center*—(providing counseling and technical assistance on a one-to-one basis for existing and potential businessmen).
    b) *A Placement Center*—(which acts as a broker between minority job-seekers and large white corporations).
    c) *An Educational Clearing House*—(which operates an educational aid fund, a college assistance program, an educational opportunities exchange, and a university liaison service).
    d) *A Research and Consultant Service*—(which conducts area research and proposes solutions to community problems).
11. *Progress Enterprises*—the entrepreneurial equivalent in Philadelphia, Pa., of the employment-oriented Opportunities Industrialization Center (OIC).

12. *Progress Association for Economic Development*—the extension of the idea of Progress Enterprises to urban areas other than Philadelphia, providing assistance to black entrepreneurship by providing:
    a) Instruction and counseling in accounting, management, and other subjects necessary for effective enterprise operations.
    b) Financial assistance.
    c) Facilities for housing business enterprises (e.g., shopping centers).

13. *Harlem Commonwealth Council*—a business-oriented group of economists, systems analysts, business planners, and others, whose objective it is to control the sources of wealth for New York's Harlem community and to assure that the wealth generated by these sources remains in the community.

14. *Foundation for Community Development*—a nonprofit corporation established in Durham, N.C. Under a $900,000 grant from OEO, a community-owned and community-controlled "for-profit" enterprise—United Durham, Inc.,—has been set up.

15. *Association to Assist Negro Businesses*—a New York City organization providing credit for black businessmen, under a mechanism whereby pledges of $10,000 were solicited from each of twenty-nine white businessmen and this used as a basis for a $290,000 line of credit for ten years to be used against loan guarantees made by AANB to black enterprises.

16. *Bedford-Stuyvesant Restoration Corporation*—seeks to:
    a) Attract and bring in capital and effort for economic development.
    b) Create business opportunities along with jobs.

c) Give residents of the area a controlling voice in affairs that will affect the future.
d) Develop programs which may be continued by the residents without external assistance.
e) Plan each project as a part of the total effort.

17. *The International Council of Shopping Centers*—a New York City-based organization offering advice and counsel on minority shopping center development.

18. *Capital Formation*—this New York City-based interracial organization teaches minority entrepreneurs where to go to get money and how to go about getting it.

19. *Fairmicco Corporation*—a joint effort, in Washington, D. C., of the Model Inner City Community Organization and the Fairchild Hiller Corporation.

20. *Arcata National Corporation*—a Menlo Park, (Calif.) corporation whose directors have established a subsidiary (i.e., Arcata Investment Company) to make high-risk loans to launch small-size and medium-size minority enterprises.

21. *"Two Plus You" Program*—established by International Industries, Inc., of Beverly Hills, California, to bring into the franchise system minority group members who would otherwise have no economic possibility of becoming a franchised entrepreneur. The "Two Plus You" concept involves a 2% down payment, after a candidate has been selected for training by the manpower staff and has completed a comprehensive training program, and "a deep emotional commitment" on the part of the candidate.

22. *The Ford Foundation*—an investment capital program relevant to the program side of the effort to develop conditions and preconditions for minority entrepreneurship and for self-help in disadvantaged areas.

23. *The Menswear Retailers of America*—a 3300-member national trade association which has committed both money and talent in a joint program with leading manufacturers to create business ownership opportunities for minority group members.

24. *The National Business League*—established by Booker T. Washington in 1900, the NBL has been in the vanguard of the struggle to propel black entrepreneurship into the mainstream of the free-enterprise system of this country for seven decades. With chapters throughout the country, its membership includes a highly diversified segment of the black business community. Its well-rounded package of services assists existing and prospective black entrepreneurs in obtaining financing to expand or begin an enterprise.

25. *Minority Contractors' Assistance Program*—a program based in Washington, D.C., designed to provide financing and assistance in meeting bonding requirements to minority contractors.

26. *Opportunity Funding Corporation*—based in Washington, D.C., this corporation seeks to provide financial, technical, and other types of assistance needed by minority entrepreneurs.

Appendix C

Blacks in Nixon Administration, 1974

The White House

Calhoun, John
Staff Assistant to the President
Scott, Stanley S.
Special Assistant to the President

Department of Agriculture

Bostic, James E., Jr. (Dr.)
Deputy Assistant Secretary for Rural Development
Schuman, Jerome
Director, Office of Equal Opportunity
Washington, Miles S., Jr.
Deputy Director, Office of Equal Opportunity

Department of Commerce

Cornelius, Samuel J.
Deputy Director
Office of Minority Business Enterprise

Parker, Lutrelle Fleming
Examiner-In-Chief
Board of Appeals, U.S. Patent Office

Department of Defense

Cowan, James R. (Dr.)
Assistant Secretary of Defense for Health and Environment
Francis, H. Minton
Deputy Assistant Secretary of Defense for Equal Opportunity (Manpower and Reserve Affairs)
James, Daniel (Chappie), Jr.
Lieutenant General, USAF
Principal Deputy Assistant Secretary of Defense for Public Affairs

Department of Health, Education, and Welfare

Coker, Irving
Deputy Assistant Secretary for Administration
Costa, John Lewis
Commissioner
Assistant Payments Administration Service
Holloway, Ruth Love (Mrs.)
Director, Right to Read Program
Thomas, Stanley B., Jr.
Assistant Secretary for Human Development
Wheeler, Robert R.
Associate Commissioner for Elementary and Secondary Education

Department of Housing and Urban Development

Britton, Theodore R., Jr.
Deputy Assistant Secretary for Policy Development and Research
Crawford, H. R.
Assistant Secretary for Housing Management
Graves, Clifford W.

Deputy Assistant Secretary for Community Planning and Management
Jenkins, Thomas O.
Deputy Assistant Secretary for Equal Opportunity (Acting)
Toote, Gloria E. A. (Dr.)
Assistant Secretary for Equal Opportunity
Williams, Paul
Director, Office of Administrative and Program Services, Housing Management

Department of the Interior
Shelton, Edward E.
Director, Office for Equal Opportunity

Department of Justice
Coleman, Frederick M.
United States Attorney
Ohio North
Crawford, Curtis C.
Member, U.S. Parole Board
Holman, Benjamin F.
Director, Community Relations Service
Jones, Donald W.
Deputy Director, Community Relations Service
Lafontant, Jewel (Mrs.)
Deputy Solicitor General
Paige, Louis S.
Chief, Fraud Section
Civil Division
Webb, Horace
Deputy Director
Office of Public Information

Department of Labor

Davis, Philip J.
Director, Office of Federal Contract Compliance and Deputy Assistant Secretary
Washington, Bennetta B. (Dr.)
Associate Director for Women's Programs & Education, Job Corps, Manpower Administration

Department of State

Fox, Richard K., Jr.
Deputy Assistant for Educational and Cultural Affairs

Agency for International Development

Adams, Samuel C., Jr.
Assistant Administrator for Africa
Davis, Hermon S.
Mission Director, Zaire Republic
Ford, William R.
Mission Director, Nigeria
Ingram, Reginald K., Sr.
Deputy Mission Director, Ghana
Johnson, Vernon C.
Mission Director, Tanzania

Ambassadors

Aggrey, O. Rudolph
Ambassador
Senegal and Gambia
Bolen, David B.
Ambassador
Botswana and Lesotho
Carter, W. Beverly, Jr.
Ambassador
Tanzania
Ferguson, C. Clyde
United States Representative

United Nations Economic and Social Council
Reinhardt, John E.
Ambassador
Nigeria
Todman, Terence
Ambassador
Guinea
White, Barbara
Alternate Representative to the United Nations for Special Political Affairs

United Nations Educational, Scientific and Cultural Organization (UNESCO)

Jones, William B.
Permanent U.S. Representative to UNESCO

United States Information Agency

Haley, George W.
Assistant Director for Equal Employment Opportunity

Department of Transportation

Banks, Calvin D.
Chief, Community Planning Assistance Division
Davis, Benjamin O., Jr.
Assistant Secretary for Environment, Safety, and Consumer Affairs
Frazier, James
Director, Office of Civil Rights
Payton, Sallyanne
Chief Counsel
Urban Mass Transportation Administration (UMTA)

Department of the Treasury

Brooks, Ronald B.
Executive Assistant to the Secretary

INDEPENDENT AGENCIES AND COMMISSIONS

Action

Bell, Andrew J.
Regional Director, Africa
Singletary, Samuel P.
Assistant Director for Minority Affairs

VISTA

Williams, Frank E.
Deputy Associate Director for VISTA and Anti-Poverty Programs

National Advisory Council on the Education of Disadvantaged Children

Crim, Alonzo A.
Member
Jenkins, Elaine B. (Mrs.)
Member

National Aeronautics and Space Administration

Jenkins, Harriett G. (Dr.)
Deputy Assistant Administrator for Equal Opportunity Programs
McConnell, Dudley G. (Dr.)
Assistant Administrator for Equal Opportunity Programs

Commission on Civil Rights

Buggs, John A.
Staff Director

Consumer Product Safety Commission

Newman, Constance E. (Mrs.)
Commissioner

District of Columbia Government

Washington, Walter E.
Mayor—Commissioner

District of Columbia Public Service Commission
Neely, H. Mason
Commissioner and Acting Chairman

Office of Economic Opportunity
Reid, Arthur Joseph
Deputy General Counsel
Walker, William L.
Regional Director, Atlanta (Region 4)
Watson, Robert Dean
General Counsel, Kansas City (Region 7)

Equal Employment Opportunity Commission
Humphrey, Melvin
Director of Research
Lewis, Colston A.
Commissioner
Powell, John H., Jr.
Chairman
Sweeney, Al
Director of Public Affairs

Federal Communications Commission
Hooks, Benjamin L.
Commissioner

Federal Reserve System
Brimmer, Andrew F. (resigned)
Member, Board of Governors

National Labor Relations Board
Jenkins, Howard, Jr.
Board Member

National Library of Medicine, Public Health Service
Smith, Eddie G., Jr. (Dr.) (Pending Confirmation)
Member, Board of Regents

Renegotiation Board
Houston, Norman B.
Board Member

Small Business Administration
Grant, Carl E.
Director of Personnel
Higgins, Connie Mack
Assistant Administrator for Minority Enterprise

United States Tariff Commission
Young, Jefferson Banks
Commissioner

Military Officers

Service		Rank
Army	Frederick F. Davidson Commanding General 8th Infantry Division United States Army Europe	Major General
	James F. Hamlet Commanding General 4th Infantry Division (Mech) & Fort Carson	Major General
	Julius W. Becton, Jr. Deputy Commanding General United States Army Training Center (Inf)	Brigadier General
	Harry W. Brooks, Jr. Assistant Division Commander 2d Infantry Division Eighth United States Army	Brigadier General
	Roscoe C. Cartwright Assistant Division Commander	Brigadier General

	3d Infantry Division United States Army Europe	
	Oliver W. Dillard Headquarters Continental Army Command	Brigadier General
	Edward Greer Deputy Commanding General United States Army Training Center (Engr)	Brigadier General
	Arthur J. Gregg Commander European Exchange System	Brigadier General
	Roscoe Robinson, Jr. Commanding General 2d Brigade 82d Airborne Division	Brigadier General
	Charles C. Rogers Commanding General 42d Field Artillery Group	Brigadier General
	Fred C. Sheffey, Jr. Chief, Finance Resources Division Director of Supplies and Maintenance Office of the Deputy Chief of Staff for Logistics	Brigadier General
	George M. Shuffer, Jr. Assistant Deputy Chief of Staff for Personnel United States Army Europe Seventh Army	Brigadier General
U.S. Army Reserve	Benjamin L. Hunton	Brigadier General
National Guard	Cunningham Bryant (D.C. ARNG)	Brigadier General

Navy	Samuel L. Gravely Commander Cruiser-Destroyer Group Two	Rear Admiral
	Gerald E. Thomas Captain	Rear Admiral (Selectee)

Air Force	Daniel James, Jr.
	Principal Deputy Assistant
	  Secretary of Defense
	  (Public Affairs)
		Lieutenant General

	Thomas E. Clifford Wing Commander 52d Tactical Fighter Wing	Brigadier General

	Lucius Theus
	Special Assistant for Social
	  Actions to the Director of
	  Personnel Plans
		Brigadier General

	Banjamin O. Davis, Jr.
	(Retired)
	(Presently the Assistant
	  Secretary of Transportation
	  for Environment, Safety,
	  and Consumer Affairs)
		Lieutenant General

U.S. Air Force Reserve	William C. Banton II	Brigadier General

Judges

*Bryant, William B.
Judge, U.S. District Court—District of Columbia
Campbell, Robert H.
Judge, District of Columbia Superior Court
Carter, Robert L.
Judge, U.S. District Court—New York South

*Indicates appointment by a previous administration

Christian, Almeric
Judge, U.S. District Court—Virgin Islands
Draper, George
Judge, District of Columbia Superior Court
Duncan, Robert
Judge, United States Court of Military Appeals
*Fauntleroy, John D.
Judge, District of Columbia Superior Court
*Fickling, Austin L.
Judge, District of Columbia Court of Appeals
Hamilton, Eugene
Judge, District of Columbia Superior Court
Haywood, Margaret
Judge, District of Columbia Superior Court
*Higgenbotham, A. L.
Judge, U.S. District Court—Pennsylvania East
Johnson, Mormalie
Judge, District of Columbia Superior Court
*Keith, Damon J.
Judge, U.S. District Court—Michigan East
*Marshall, Thurgood
Associate Justice, United States Supreme Court
*McCree, H. Wade, Jr.
Judge, U.S. Court of Appeals—Sixth Circuit
Moore, Luke C.
Judge, District of Columbia Superior Court
*Motley, Constance Baker
Judge, U.S. District Court—New York South
Moultrie, H. Carl
Judge, District of Columbia Superior Court
Newman, Theodore
Judge, District of Columbia Superior Court
Pair, Hubert
Judge, District of Columbia Court of Appeals
Parker, Barrington
Judge, U.S. District Court—District of Columbia

*Parsons, James B.
Judge, U.S. District Court—Illinois North
Penn, John G.
Judge, District of Columbia Superior Court
Pierce, Lawrence
Judge, U.S. District Court—New York South
*Pryor, William
Judge, District of Columbia Superior Court
*Robinson, Aubrey, Jr.
Judge, U.S. District Court—District of Columbia
*Robinson, Spottswood
Judge, United States Court of Appeals
Thompson, William
Judge, District of Columbia Superior Court
*Waddy, Joseph C.
Judge, U.S. District Court—District of Columbia
Washington, James
Judge, District of Columbia Superior Court
*Watson, James L.
Judge, United States Customs Court
Williams, David
Judge, U.S. District Court—California Central

Notes

CHAPTER ONE

1. The intellectually curious may be interested in contrasting the views of, say, David Ricardo, Karl Marx, Joseph Schumpeter, John Maynard Keynes, and Jacob Viner with some of the more contemporary economists (e.g., W. Arthur Lewis, Benjamin Higgins, Walter Rostow, Roy Harrod, Alvin Hansen, W. W. Leontief, Joan Robinson, and Nicholas Kaldor).
2. Jacob Viner, *International Trade and Economic Development*, (Glencoe, Ill.: Free Press, 1952).
3. W. W. Rostow, "The Take-Off Into Self-Sustained Growth," *The Economic Journal*, 66, (March 1956).
4. Joseph A. Schumpeter, *The Theory of Economic Development* (New York: Oxford University Press, 1961), Chapters I and II.
5. Everett E. Hagen and O. I. Hawrylyshyn, "Analysis of World Income and Growth, 1955–1965," *Economic*

Development and Cultural Change (The University of Chicago Press, Volume 18, Number 1, Part II, October 1969), pp. 24 and 32.
6. Ibid. The percentages are calculations based on statistics found on pp. 12, 16, 20, 23, 28, 29, 31, and 32.
7. Schumpeter, *Theory of Economic Development,* p. 64.
8. See especially Colin Clark, *Conditions of Economic Progress,* 3rd ed. (London: Macmillan, 1957).
9. The reader will undoubtedly recognize this progression as Karl Marx's interpretation of history.
10. This is the international or balance-of-payments manifestations of the progress of an economy. See, for example, Paul A. Samuelson, *Economics: An Introductory Analysis,* Seventh Edition (New York: McGraw-Hill Book Co., 1967), pp. 636–37.
11. W. W. Rostow, *Stages of Economic Growth,* Second Edition (New York: Cambridge University Press, 1971).
12. Schumpeter, *Theory of Economic Development,* p. 64.
13. Ibid., p. 66.
14. Simon Kuznet, *Six Lectures on Economic Growth* (Glencoe, Illinois: The Free Press, 1959).
15. Schumpeter, op. cit. p. 63.
16. Ibid.
17. Karl Marx, *A Contribution to the Critique of Political Economy* (Chicago: Keri, 1904), pp. 11–13.

CHAPTER TWO

1. *Statistical Abstract of the United States, 1972* (Bureau of the Census, U.S. Department of Commerce), p. xiii. The source does not give the total nonwhite population for 1971; it was estimated at 25.9 million by applying the 1970 percentage of black population to the total nonwhite population—i.e., 88.6 percent—to the 1971 black population estimate. It should also be noted that the 88.6 percent for 1970 is significant-

ly below the 1960 figure of 92.2 percent, reflecting a greater increase during the 1960s of the Spanish-speaking nonwhite population.
2. Ibid., p. 322.
3. Ibid.
4. James Tobin, "On Improving the Economic Status of the Negro," in E. C. Budd, ed., *Inequality and Poverty* (New York: Norton, 1967), p. 195.
5. *The Social and Economic Status of Negroes in the United States, 1970,* BLS Report No. 394, and Current Population Reports, Series P–23, No. 38 (Bureau of the Census, U.S. Department of Commerce), pp. 26, 36, 38.
6. Ibid., pp. 37, 39–41.
7. For an excellent discussion of the various categories of poverty, see Anthony Downs, *Who Are The Urban Poor?*, Supplementary Paper Number 26, Committee For Economic Development, New York, 1970.
8. Alan B. Batchelder, *The Economics of Poverty* (New York: Wiley, 1971), pp. 68–69.
9. Unemployment rates for selected years were:

Year	Nonwhite	White	Ratio: Nonwhite to White
1950	9.0%	4.9%	1:8
1953	4.5	2.7	1:7
1955	8.7	3.9	2:2
1958	12.6	6.1	1:1
1960	10.2	4.9	2:1
1965	8.1	4.1	2:0
1970	8.2	4.5	1:8

Source: *The Social and Economic Status of Negroes in the United States, 1970,* op. cit., p. 48.

10. *Statistical Abstract of the United States, 1972,* pp. 217, 221, 223.
11. Everett E. Hagen, *The Economics of Development,* (Homewood, Illinois: Richard D. Irwin, 1968) pp. 40–42.

12. *Federal Reserve Bulletin,* June 1973, A64; and *Economic Report of the President,* February 1970, pp. 202 and 208.
13. *The Social and Economic Status of Negroes in the United States, 1970,* p. 61.
14. Ibid., p. 60.
15. See Dale L. Hiestand, *Discrimination in Employment— An Appraisal of the Research,* Policy Papers in Human Resources and Industrial Relations 16, a joint publication of the Institute of Labor and Industrial Relations (The University of Michigan—Wayne State University) and the National Manpower Policy Task Force, Washington, D.C., Ann Arbor, Michigan, February 1970, p. 13.
16. *The Social and Economic Status of Negroes in the United States, 1970,* p. 67.
17. *Blacks Serving in the Nixon Administration, 1974* (The White House, April 1974). See Appendix C for the complete list of names, excluding those serving the Nixon Administration on a part-time basis.
18. *The Social and Economic Status of Negroes in the United States, 1970,* p. 53.
19. Statistics on prostitution and drug abuse are difficult to obtain and often are unreliable. Illegitimacy rates per 1,000 teen-agers (i.e., 15–19 years old) are as follows for the period under review:

	1950	1960	1965	1968
Nonwhite	68.5	76.5	75.8	82.8
White	5.1	6.6	7.9	9.8

Ibid., p. 115

With respect to its statistics on illegitimacy, the reference quotes its source—i.e., the U.S. Department of Health, Education and Welfare—as follows: "No estimates are included for misstatements on the birth record or for failure to register births ... The decision to conceal the illegitimacy of births is likely conditioned by attitudes in the mother's social group towards her and towards children born out of wedlock. Also, the ability (economic or otherwise) to leave a community before the birth of a child is an important consideration. These factors probably result in proportionately greater understatement of illegitimacy in the white group than in Negro and other races ..."

20. Ibid., p. 107.
21. Ibid., p. 32.
22. Ibid., p. 71.
23. Tobin, "On Improving the Economic Status of the Negro," pp. 194–213.
24. *The Statistical Abstract of the United States, 1973*, pp. 111 and 114.
25. Ibid., p. 115.
26. Taken from a statement prepared by Dr. Thomas Pettigrew for presentation at The White House Conference on Education, July 20–21, 1965. Washington, D.C.
27. Batchelder, *Economics of Poverty*, p. 125.
28. Ibid., p. 182.
29. *The Social and Economic Status of Negroes in the United States, 1970*, p. 34.
30. Ibid., p. 77.
31. Statistics on housing—Ibid., pp. 87–91, and on maternal and infant mortality rates—p. 98. Other statistics are to be found in the *Statistical Abstract of the United States, 1972*, pp. 50–57.
32. Ibid., pp. 205–207.
33. Ibid., pp. 210–211.
34. Peter Orleans and William Russell, Jr., eds., *Race, Change, and Urban Society, Urban Affairs Annual*

Reviews, Vol. 5 (Beverly Hills, California: Sage, 1971), p. 9.
35. *The Social and Economic Status of Negroes in the United States, 1970,* pp. 13–19.
36. *Statistical Abstract of the United States, 1972,* p. 471.

CHAPTER THREE

1. W. Arthur Lewis, *The Theory of Economic Growth* (London: George Allen and Unwin Ltd., 1955), p. 11.
2. This chapter is largely an amalgamation of two lectures given by the author. The first was entitled, "Psychological Factors in Black Economic Development," presented at the *Symposium on the State of the Black Economy,* sponsored by the Chicago Economic Development Corporation, May 10–11, 1973. The second lecture, on "Black Culture and the Black Experience," was presented at the Management Education Seminar of the E. I. du Pont de Nemours, at Old Hickory, Tennessee, on November 27, 1973.
3. Kurt W. Marek, *Yestermorrow* (New York: Alfred A. Knopf, 1961), p. 77.
4. Kenneth Boulding, *The Meaning of the 20th Century* (New York: Harper and Row, 1964), p. 7.
5. Alvin Toffler, *Future Shock* (New York: Random House, 1970), pp. 15–16.
6. Ibid., pp. 11–12.
7. Ibid., pp. 3–4.
8. Lewis, *Theory of Economic Growth,* pp. 101–107.
9. H. Richard Niebahr, *The Responsible Self: An Essay in Christian Moral Philosophy* (New York: Harper and Row, 1963), Chapters 1 and 2.
10. Melville Herskovits, *The Myth of the Negro Past* (Boston: Beacon Press, 1968).
11. Article 1, Section 2, of the U.S. Constitution defined

blacks as two-thirds of a person. The Fourteenth Amendment to the Constitution repealed this Section.
12. John Hope Franklin, *Reconstruction After the Civil War* (Chicago: University of Chicago Press, 1961), pp. 154–58, and Rayford W. Logan, *The Negro in American Life and Thought: The Nadir, 1877–1901* (New York: Dial Press, 1954), pp. 239–74.
13. Steven R. Asher and Vernon L. Allen, "Racial Preference and Social Comparison Processes," *Journal of Social Issues*, XXV, No. 1 (1969).
14. *Statistical Abstract of the United States, 1972*, p. 112.
15. In 1969, according to official statistics, 3.6 percent of the black population 14 years old and above was illiterate. Ibid., p. 113.
16. *The Social and Economic Status of Negroes in the United States, 1970*, p. 93.
17. Lester C. Thurow, *Poverty and Discrimination* (Washington, D.C.: The Brookings Institution, 1969), p. 21.
18. Thurow uses the bottom 15 percent as including those who "could be impoverished regardless of actual income." This writer uses the bottom 20 percent because, for 1970, this percentage of family units received incomes of less than $4000, which is regarded as poverty-level income.
19. *Statistical Abstract of the United States, 1973* (Bureau of the Census, Social and Economic Statistics Administration, U.S. Department of Commerce), p. 328.
20. Ibid., p. 334.
21. Ibid., p. 335.
22. *The Social and Economic Status of Negroes in the United States, 1970*, pp. 25–35, No. 38, Current Population Reports, Series P-23, No. 394, pp. 25–35.
23. Lee Rainwater, "Crucible of Identity: The Negro Lower-Class Family," in *The Negro American*, Talcott Parsons and Kenneth B. Clark, eds. (Boston: Beacon

Press, 1968), p. 167. For the interested reader, Raintree's article is an excellent short "description and analysis of slum Negro family patterns as these reflect and sustain Negroes' adaptations to the economic, social and personal situation into which they are born and in which they must live."
24. *The Social and Economic Status of Negroes in the United States, 1970,* pp. 107 and 109.
25. *Search—A Report From the Urban Institute* (Washington, September-October 1973), p. 3.
26. Kerner Report, "The Escape from the Ghetto: Immigrants and Blacks," in *The Economics of Black America,* eds., Harold C. Vatter and Thomas Palm (New York: Harcourt, 1972), p. 55.
27. L. C. Thurow, *Poverty and Discrimination,* pp. 117-25. See also Flournoy A. Coles, Jr., "The Economics of Minorities," *The Negro Educational Review,* Vol. XXIV, Nos. 1 and 2. (January-April, 1973).
28. For example, see Marcus Alexis, "Consumption by the Poor," a paper presented at the Conference on Research on Urban Poverty, sponsored by the Social Science Research Council, the Woodrow Wilson School, and the Industrial Relations Section, Princeton University, May 23, 1969; David Caplovitz, *The Poor Pay More* (New York: The Free Press, 1963); the studies conducted by the Federal Trade Commission on the retail business in Washington, D. C.; and the Kerner Commission Report on urban disturbances during the mid-sixties.
29. St. Clair Drake, "The Social and Economic Status of the Negro in the United States," in *The Negro Americans,* eds., Talcott Parsons and Kenneth B. Clark (Boston: Beacon, 1968), p. 5. See also Lloyd W. Warner and Allison Davis, "A Comparative Study of American Caste," in *Race Relations and the Race Problem,* ed., Edgar Thomas (Raleigh, N.C., 1939).

30. *The Social and Economic Status of Negroes in the United States, 1970,* op. cit., p. 34.
31. Leonard Goodwin, *Do the Poor Want to Work?* (Washington, D.C.: The Brookings Institution, 1972), pp. 113–118. See also Goodwin's "Welfare Mothers and the Work Ethic," *Monthly Labor Review,* Bureau of Labor Statistics, U.S. Department of Labor, August 1972, pp. 35–37.
32. Edward Simpkins, "The Work Ethic Is Not Enough," *Monthly Labor Reivew,* Bureau of Labor Statistics, U.S. Department of Labor, April 1973, pp. 59–60.
33. See, for example, *The Social and Economic Status of Negroes in the United States, 1969.* Bureau of Labor Statistics (U.S. Department of Labor) and Bureau of the Census (U.S. Department of Commerce), BLS Report No. 375, p. 20.
34. St. Clair Drake, "The Social and Economic Status of the Negro in the United States," in *The Negro American,* p. 5.

CHAPTER FOUR

1. All statistics used in this section are to be found in the *Statistical Abstract of the United States, 1973,* U. S. Bureau of the Census, unless otherwise noted.
2. *Federal Reserve Bulletin, May 1974.* Board of Governors, Federal Reserve System, A54.
3. Robert J. Lampman, "Changes in the Concentration of Wealth," in *Inequality and Poverty,* ed., Edward C. Budd (New York: W. W. Norton, 1967), p. 81.
4. Dorothy S. Projector and Gertrude S. Weiss, "The Distribution of Wealth in 1962," in *Inequality and Poverty,* p. 88.
5. For some details on the extent of black ownership of land in the latter part of the nineteenth century, for example, see Booker T. Washington, *The Story of the*

Negro (New York: Doubleday, 1909); "Negro Settlements in Ohio and the Northwest Territory" (Chapter XLL, Volume I), and "The Rise of the Negro Land-owner" (Chapter II, Volume II).
6. *The Social and Economic Status of Negroes in the United States, 1970,* p. 26.
7. *Mobility in the Negro Community: Guidelines for Research on Social and Economic Progress,* Clearinghouse Publication No. 11 (U.S. Civil Rights Commission, June 1968).
8. *The Annals: The Negro Protest,* Vol. 357, January 1965, p. ix.
9. Alan B. Batchelder, "Economic Forces Serving the Ends of the Negro Protest," Ibid., pp. 80–88.
10. Clifton R. Wharton, Jr., "Reflections on Black Intellectual Power," in *State of the Black Economy,* ed., Gerald F. Whittaker (East Lansing, Mich.: Michigan State University Press, 1973), p. 19.
11. Ibid., p. 11.
12. A more rational program of assistance to the predominantly black institutions may involve closing down the more marginal ones or merging them with other institutions. Despite their undeniable contributions to the development of black people in the past, it is becoming increasingly difficult to justify—on economic or other grounds—the continued existence of all the black colleges now operating.
13. Such programs have been and are being operated, for example, by the American Economic Association and the United Negro College Fund.
14. In Nashville, for example, students enrolled at Fisk University, Meharry Medical College, Vanderbilt University, Peabody College, and Scarritt College are permitted to take courses at any of the other four colleges without additional charge.
15. The Graduate School of Management of Vanderbilt Uni-

versity and the Department of Economics and Business Administration of Fisk University are currently finalizing such a "3–2" program. With specific reference to schools offering financial assistance to minority students in the areas of business and management, see *Higher Education For Minority Business* (U.S. Department of Commerce, Office of Minority Business Enterprise, April 1970), pp. 1–87.
16. The "cluster" concept, sponsored by the National Alliance of Businessmen, provides for technical and other assistance to selected predominantly black colleges through the cooperative efforts of several corporations.
17. *The Social and Economic Status of Negroes in the United States, 1970,* op. cit., p. 83.
18. Wharton, *State of the Black Economy,* op. cit., p. 9.
19. Ibid., pp. 10–11.
20. *Statistical Abstract of the United States, 1973,* op. cit., p. 123.
21. Ibid., p. 138.
22. For details on how such cooperation can be effected, see the Report of the Forty-third American Assembly on "The Changing World of Work," November 1–4, 1973, Columbia University. The full report is scheduled to be printed for the public under the title *The Worker and the Job: Coping with Change,* by Prentice-Hall, Inc., in the winter of 1974.
23. Everett E. Hagen, *The Economics of Development,* (Homewood, Illinois: Richard D. Irwin, 1968), pp. 40–41.
24. *Federal Reserve Bulletin, June 1973,* A64 and A68; and *Economic Report of the President, February 1970,* p. 202.
25. *Economic Report of the President,* p. 186.
26. *Admission and Apprenticeship in the Building Trades,* Labor Management Services Administration, U.S.

Department of Labor (Washington, D.C.: U.S. Government Printing Office, 1971). Data on race are to be found in publications of the Bureau of Apprenticeship Training, U.S. Department of Labor.
27. For example, see Richard L. Rowan, and Lester Rubin, *Opening Up the Skilled Construction Trades to Blacks: A Study of the Washington and Indianapolis Plans for Minority Employment* (Philadelphia: Industrial Research Unit, Wharton School of Finance and Commerce, University of Pennsylvania, 1972).
28. Report of the Forty-third American Assembly, op. cit., p. 9.
29. Robert J. Lampman, "Income Distribution and Poverty" in *Poverty in America*, ed., Margaret S. Gordon (San Francisco: Chandler, 1965), pp. 109–113.
30. Edwin M. Epstein and David R. Hampton, eds., "Exploitation of Disadvantaged Consumers by Retail Merchants," in *Black Americans and White Business*, eds., Edwin M. Epstein and David R. Hampton (Encino and Belmont, California: Dickenson Publishing, 1971), p. 174.
31. David Caplovitz, "Consumer Problems: Shady Sales Practices," ibid., pp. 177–185.
32. "Consumer Credit and the Poor," ibid., pp. 189–194.
33. *1970 Census, Volume 5, Census of Housing*, Bureau of the Census, U.S. Department of Commerce.
34. See the series of articles written by Leonard Downie for the *Washington Post*, January 5–14, 1969.
35. See, for example, Marcus Alexis, "Some Negro-White Differences in Consumption," *The American Journal of Economics and Sociology*, Vol. 21, (January 1962), pp. 11–28.
36. Statistics taken from *Black Enterprise* (New York: Earl G. Graves Publishing, June 1973).

37. *Fortune,* May 1972.
38. *Fortune,* July 1973.
39. Richard F. America, Jr., "What Do You People Want?" *Harvard Business Review,* Vol. 47, No. 2 (March-April 1969), pp. 103–112.
40. H. W. Johnson, "Management for the 70's," *Dun's Review,* 1968, p. 19.
41. Joseph A. Schumpeter, *The Theory of Economic Development,* (New York: Oxford University Press, 1961), Chapter II.
42. For a very thorough discussion, see Moriuemon Ito, *The Role of Entrepreneurship in Economic Development* (Honolulu, Hawaii: Technology and Development Institute, East-West Center, Working Paper Series No. 6).
43. Charles J. Stokes, *Managerial Economics: A Textbook on the Economics of Management* (New York: Random House, 1969), p. 176.
44. Joseph A. Schumpeter, *op. cit.,* p. 66.
45. H. G. Barnett, *Innovation: The Basis of Cultural Change* (New York: McGraw-Hill, 1953).
46. George M. Foster, *Traditional Cultures and Impact of Technological Change* (New York: Harper, 1962).
47. K. J. Davey, *Decision Making,* (Lagos, Nigeria: The African Association for Public Administration and Management, AAPAM Reprint 2), p. 4.
48. Documentation for this assertion is to be found in *Statistical Abstract of the United States, 1971,* pp. 221, 223, 233–35, and 290. *The Social and Economic Status of Negroes in the United States, 1970,* op. cit., pp. 61 and 65; and Armand J. Thiebolt, *Negro Employment in Basic Industry* and Linda P. Fletcher, *Negro Employment in Finance* (Philadelphia: University of Pennsylvania, 1970).

CHAPTER FIVE

1. E. Franklin Frazier, *Black Bourgeoisie*, (Glencoe, Illinois: The Free Press, 1957). The National Negro Business League has recently been renamed the National Business League.
2. Andrew F. Brimmer, "Small Business and Economic Development in the Negro Community," in *Black Americans and White Business*, eds., Edwin M. Epstein and David R. Hampton (Encino and Belmont, California: Dickenson Publishing Company, 1971), pp. 265–275.
3. Unless otherwise noted, this section is an amalgamation of parts of two previous publications of the author— i.e., "Financial Institutions and Black Entrepreneurship," *Journal of Black Studies* (Beverly Hills, California: Sage Publications, March 1973), Vol. 3, No. 3, pp. 329–331; and "The Unique Problems of the Black Businessman," *Vanderbilt Law Review* (Nashville, Tennessee: The Law School, Vanderbilt University, April 1973), Vol. 26, No. 3, pp. 509–512.
4. Article I, Section 2, of the U.S. Constitution (1788): "Representatives and direct Taxes shall be apportioned among the several States which may be included within this Union, according to their respective Numbers, which shall be determined by adding the whole Numbers of free Persons, including those bound to Service for a Term of Years, and excluding Indians not taxed, three fifths of all other Persons." This was subsequently repealed by Article XIV, Section 2.
5. Berkeley G. Burrell, and John Seder, *Getting It Together: Black Businessmen in America* (New York: Harcourt, 1971), pp. 7–8.
6. Ibid., p. 8.
7. These figures were transcribed by the author from offi-

cial census reports of 1890, and 1900, located at the Bureau of the Census, U.S. Department of Commerce.
8. W. E. B. DuBois, *The Negro in Business* (Atlanta, Georgia: Atlanta University, reprinted 1968).
9. Booker T. Washington, *The Story of the Negro: The Rise of the Race from Slavery* (New York: Doubleday, 1909), Volume II, pp. 190–210.
10. Burrell and Seder, *Getting It Together*, pp. 21–24.
11. Washington, *The Story of the Negro*, Chapter IX.
12. Ibid., p. 215.
13. Ibid., p. 148.
14. *Statistical Abstract of the United States,* 1973, p. 474.
15. Data on receipts and numbers of firms to be found in *Statistical Abstract of the United States, 1972,* p. 471.
16. *SBA Economic Review,* Small Business Administration, 1972.
17. Flournoy A. Coles, Jr., *An Analysis of Black Entrepreneurship in Seven Urban Areas* (Washington, D.C.: National Urban League, November, 1969).
18. See, for example, *Black Enterprise* (New York: Earl G. Graves, Ltd., June 1973), Vol. 3, No. 11.
19. Dun and Bradstreet, Inc., *Patterns for Success in Managing a Business* (Dun and Bradstreet Series No. 2, Business Education Division, 1967).
20. Eugene Foley, "The Negro Businessman in Search of a Tradition," in *The Negro American,* eds., Talcott Parsons and Kenneth B. Clark (Boston: Beacon Press, 1966), pp. 555–579.
21. The enabling legislation is the Public Works and Economic Development Act of 1965, which also authorizes the EDA to make long-term, low-interest loans to qualifying industrial companies for the purchase and development of land and facilities, including machinery and equipment.

22. In Executive Order No. 11458, which created the Office of Minority Business Enterprise, President Nixon gave the Secretary of Commerce a broad mandate to coordinate the various federal agencies and programs dealing with the problems of minority entrepreneurs toward a national program for minority business enterprise. In Executive Order No. 11518, the president, pursuant to the Small Business Act, also provided for increased representation of the interests of small businesses before federal government agencies and directed that the Small Business Administration "particularly consider the needs and interests of minority-owned small business concerns and of members of minority groups seeking entry into the business community."
23. See Manpower Development and Training Act of 1962.
24. The Model Cities program, begun under the Demonstration Cities and Metropolitan Development Act of 1966, established city demonstration agencies to concentrate governmental and private efforts in designated Model Cities areas. These programs have been curtailed, rather drastically in some instances.
25. See Uniform Relocation Assistance and Real Property Acquisition Policies Act of 1970.
26. Title I–D of the Economic Opportunity Act of 1964.
27. The Service Corps of Retired Executives (SCORE) was established in 1964.
28. Under this program, the SBA guarantees the lease payments of a small business.
29. Often called the "Section 502" program.
30. The MESBIC is a subsequent development to the Small Business Investment Company (SBIC). Although several provisions facilitated SBIC financing of businesses in low-income areas, none provided a significant incentive. A proposed regulation that would have permitted the SBA to guarantee 90 percent of

SBIC loans made to disadvantaged owners' businesses was rejected. As an alternative, the Office of Minority Business Enterprise sought to recruit private sources of capital to form MESBICs. MESBICs represent the principal innovation by the Nixon Administration to encourage minority business development. See generally Office of Minority Business Enterprise, U.S. Department of Commerce, MESBICs and Minority Enterprise (1971); Nadau, "Effective MESBIC Organization," 27 Bus. Law 665 (1972); Rosenbloom & Shank, "Let's Write Off MESBICs," 48 Harvard Business Review 90 (September-October 1970).
31. Operation Business Mainstream was created in late 1969.
32. To be eligible for an 8(a) subcontract, "a concern must be owned or destined to be owned by socially or economically disadvantaged persons. This category often includes, but is not restricted to, Black Americans, American Indians, Spanish Americans, Oriental Americans, Eskimos and Aleuts." Recent federal cases have upheld the 8(a) program against attacks on its legality. See Ray Baillie Trash Hauling, Inc., v. Kleppe, 41 U.S.L.Q. 2373 (5th Cir., January 5, 1973), rev'g 334 F. Supp. 194, 202 (S.D. Fla. 1971); Fortec Constructors v. Kleppe, 350 F. Supp. 171, 173 (D.D.C. 1972). For a discussion of the constitutionality of "compensatory" or "preferential" treatment of minorities see Elden, "Forty Acres and a Mule," with Interest: The Constitutionality of Black Capitalism, Benign School Quotas, and Other Statutory Racial Classifications, 47 J. Urban L. 591 (1969).
33. These are the so-called "7(a)" business loans. Generally, conservative investment policy became the principal rule for allocating 7(a) funds, with the result that the low-income borrower suffered a disadvantage.

34. Subchapter IV of the Economic Opportunity Act is the authority for these loans.
35. Information provided by SBA Regional Office, Nashville, Tennessee.
36. Information provided by Reports Management Division, SBA, Washington, D.C.
37. *Statistical Abstract of the United States,* 1973, op. cit.
38. See "Small Firms to Get Boost Into Exporting From Giants," *Commerce Today,* Volume 3, (February 5, 1973), p. 38.
39. For example, see *New Business Opportunities,* General Electric, Issue 4/1973.
40. See "Larger Firms Prove Best Market for Sales by Minority Enterprises," *Commerce Today,* Volume 3 (April 16, 1973), pp. 13-15.
41. For a complete listing, see *Franchise Company Data,* Bureau of Domestic Commerce, U.S. Department of Commerce (December 1970).
42. This program is sponsored by the Manpower Administration of the U.S. Department of Labor.
43. For a more detailed description of the program, see "Management Assistance for the Small Businessman: A Joint Program of SBA and the University," *Journal of Small Business Management,* Volume 12, Number 1 (January 1974), pp. 6-12. For a list of schools offering special programs to aid minority business, see *Higher Education Aid for Minority Business* (U.S. Department of Commerce, Office of Minority Business Enterprise, April 1970) pp. 88-95.
44. *ACCESS* (Washington, D.C.: U.S. Department of Commerce, Office of Minority Business Enterprise, January/February 1974). An extremely noteworthy program, for example, is the cooperative Business Management Fellowship Program (BMFP) of the Office of Minority Business Enterprise and the Na-

tional Football League, in its second year, which is designed "to help introduce private industry to a unique business training program for disadvantaged young people." A total of 508 fellowships were awarded to young people in 1953, and 100 corporations participated in the program. The 1974 goals are 1000 fellowships and 200 participating corporations (*ACCESS* March/April 1974).
45. *Minority Enterprise and Expanded Ownership: Blueprint for the 70's,* Report of the President's National Advisory Council on Minority Enterprise, June 1971, Chapter IV.
46. Ibid., p. 5.
47. Presidential Message to the Congress, March 20, 1970.
48. Presidential Message to the Congress, October 13, 1971. This message was accompanied by a proposal that funding for the Office of Minority Business Enterprise be increased by $100 million—i.e., from $3.6 million to $43.6 million in fiscal year 1972, and from $3.6 million to $63.6 million in fiscal year 1973.
49. R. P. Black, and D. E. Harless, *Nonbank Financial Institutions* (Federal Reserve Bank of Richmond, December 1969). The assets of the institutions at the end of 1967 were:

Type of Institution	Assets (in billions of dollars)
Life insurance companies	$ 77.4
Savings and loan associations	143.6
Pension funds	71.8
Mutual savings banks	66.4
Investment companies	48.5
Property-casualty insurance companies	46.6
Sales and consumer finance companies	36.6
Credit unions	12.7

50. *ACCESS,* op. cit.

CHAPTER SIX

1. Profit maximization is, of course, related to the marginal productivity theory. The author is cognizant of recent criticisms of the theory as an adequate explanation for employer behavior in that many employers may be motivated by such noneconomic considerations as the desire for power and/or prestige. Under such conditions, the critics contend, the level of profit sought may be based on a fair return on investment, which may be less than the maximum profit earnable. Nevertheless, the author believes that the pursuit of long-term profit maximization explains the behavior of most businessmen, and that the marginal productivity theory is logically deduced from that motivation.
2. *Facts About Blacks, 1974* (Los Angeles: Jeffries and Associates, Inc.)
3. *Ebony* (Chicago: Johnson Publishing Company, Inc., December 1973–April 1974).
4. *Statistical Abstract of the United States, 1973*, p. 471.
5. Ibid., p. 472.
6. Ibid., p. 479.
7. Ibid., pp. 481–482.
8. Ibid.
9. Ibid.
10. Richard Kaufman, "We Must Guard Against Unwarranted Influence by the Military-Industrial Complex," *The New York Times Magazine*, June 22, 1969.
11. R. Oliver, "The Employment Effects of Defense Expenditures," *Monthly Labor Review*, September 1967, pp. 10–11.
12. See, for example, Everett E. Hagen, *The Economics of Development* (Homewood, Illinois: Richard D. Irwin, Inc., 1968), pp. 188–192 and Chapter 11; E. A. G. Robinson, ed., *Economic Consequences of the Size*

of Nations (New York: St. Martin's Press, 1960); and Livingston, ed., *Economic Policy for Development* (Baltimore, Maryland: Penguin Books, Inc., 1971), pp. 138-139, 144, 165, 268-269, 427, and 434. Hagen lists education and training of the labor force and pure technical advance as the two other elements of importance in the residual (p. 190).
13. Kenneth E. Boulding, "Is Economics Culture-Bound?" in *The Economics of Black America*, Harold G. Vatter, and Thomas Palm, eds., (New York: Harcourt Brace, 1972), p. 33.
14. Thomas Palm, "The Limitations of Standard Theory," ibid., pp. 35-6.
15. Four theories are examined in some detail because of their presumed applicability to economic development generally speaking. In addition, less-general theories that appear to have some meaning for black economic development are briefly surveyed in terms of their major elements.
16. Benjamin Higgins, *Economic Development: Principles, Problems, and Policies* (New York: W. W. Norton, 1959) pp. 87-94.
17. T. S. Malthus, *Principles of Political Economy (1820)*.
18. Marxist theory of economic development, to the extent it can be termed such, is to be found throughout *Das Kapital*, as opposed to being localized in a particular chapter or volume. Several attempts have been made to summarize the theory; however, the current author has found three of these summaries to be particularly helpful. They are Higgins, op. cit. pp. 107-121; John E. Elliot, *Comparative Economic Systems* (Englewood Cliffs, N.J.: Prentice-Hall, 1973), pp. 107-151; and Eric Roll, *A History of Economic Thought* (Englewood Cliffs, N.J.: Prentice-Hall, Inc., 1942), pp. 315-324.
19. Paul Baran, and Paul Sweezy, "Monopoly Capitalism and

Race Relations," in *Up Against the American Myth*, eds., Tom Christofel, David Finkelhor, and Dan Gilbarg (New York: Holt, 1970), pp. 277–290.
20. For distinctions between these three forms of Socialism, see Elliott, *Comparative Economic Systems*, Chapters 10, 11 and 14.
21. Joseph A. Schumpeter, *Theory of Economic Development* (Cambridge, Massachusetts: Harvard University Press, 1934), and *Business Cycles* (New York: McGraw-Hill, 1939).
22. Henry C. Wallich, "Some Notes Towards a Theory of Derived Development," in *The Economics of Underdevelopment*, eds., A. N. Agarwala and G. P. Singh (New York: Oxford University Press, 1963), pp. 189–204.
23. Higgins, *Economic Development*, Chapters 6–7.
24. Hans W. Singer, "The Mechanics of Economic Development," in *The Economics of Underdevelopment*, op. cit., pp. 381–399.
25. Walter W. Rostow, *The Stages of Economic Growth* (Cambridge, The University Press, 1961).
26. P. N. Rosenstein-Rodan, "Programming and Theory in Italian Practice," *Investment Criteria and Economic Growth* (Cambridge, Massachusetts, 1955). For various views on balanced v. unbalanced growth, see also Ragnar Nurkse, *Problems of Capital Formation in Underdeveloped Countries* (New York: Oxford, 1953), Chapter I; Hans W. Singer, "The Concept of Balanced Growth and Economic Development: Theory and Facts," University of Texas Conference on Economic Development, April, 1958, pp. 4 and 6; Albert Hirschman, *The Strategy of Economic Development* (New Haven: Yale University Press, 1958), p. 36; and W. Arthur Lewis, *The Theory of Economic Growth* (London: George Allen & Unwin Ltd., 1955), pp. 276–283.

27. The author is of the opinion that it would probably be best not to attempt a matching arrangement between black savings and white inputs, because of varying attitudes, financial capabilities, and other variables.
28. Hagen, *The Economics of Development,* p. 192.
29. Ibid., pp. 211–13.

Index

Alexis, Marcus, 201, 206
Alienation, 47–48
Allen, Vernon L., 44, 200
America, Richard F., Jr., 88–89, 159, 206
American Academy of Political and Social Science, 71
American Assembly, report on equal employment opportunities, 80–81, 205
Asher, Steven R., 44, 200
Association for the Integration of Management, 80

Baran, Paul, 149, 216
Barnet, H. G., 207
Batchelder, Alan B., 16, 26, 195, 198, 203
Black business enterprise, 33, 36
  current status, 107–11
  federal assistance to, 112–24 (*see also* Appendix A)
  history of, 102–7
  improvement and expansion of, 111–32
  private assistance to, 101, 115–20, 122–24 (*see also* Appendix B)
  size of units of, 139–43
Black economic development
  alertness to opportunities, 188–94
  an approach to, 158–61
  financial availabilities for, 126–30
  goals of, 67–68, 70, 99
  management of, 89–90
  planning for, 61-62, 99
  qualitative changes in, 12, 71–72

role of religion in, 40–41
technological progress in, 161–63
Black, R. P., 112
Black Separatism, 47
Boulding, Kenneth, 38, 146, 199
Brimmer, Andrew F., 102, 207
Burrell, Berkeley G., 208

Capital accumulation, 158–61
Caplovitz, David, 83, 201, 207
Carmichael, Stokely, 44
Center for Democratic Studies, 81–82
Civil Rights Act (1964), 79
Clark, Colin, 194
Clark, Kenneth B., 44, 200, 201
Coles, Flournoy A., Jr., 110, 201, 207–8, 209
Community development corporations, 97–98, 113
Compensatory consumption, 48–50
Consumer knowledge, 83–86
Corporate America, and black economic development, 136–40

Davey, K. J., 93, 207
Davis, Allison, 201
Department of Minority Economic Development, 98–100, 129, 159, 162–63, 165
Downs, Anthony, 195
Drake, St. Clair, 56, 201, 202
Du Bois, W. E. B., 105, 208

Education, 19–20, 24-28, 40, 52, 57
improvements in, 34–35
in predominantly black colleges, 73–75
Elliott, John, 216
Employment, 17–21, 34, 52, 55, 58, 71
Epstein, Edwin M., 205
Equal Employment Opportunity Commission, 79

Fletcher, Linda P., 207
Foley, Eugene, 112, 209
Foster, George M., 92, 207
Franklin, John Hope, 199
Frazier, E. Franklin, 101–2, 207

Ginzberg, Eli, 70
Goodwin, Leonard, 58, 202

Hagen, Everett E., 77, 164, 194, 196, 205, 217
Hamilton, Charles, 44
Hampton, David R., 205
Hansen, Alvin, 154–55, 193
Harless, D. E., 213
Harrington, Michael, 81
Harrod, Roy, 154–55, 193
Hawrylyshyn, O. I., 194
Herskovits, Melville, 42, 199
Hiestand, Dale L., 70, 196
Higgins, Benjamin, 193, 216
Hirschman, Albert, 217
Housing, 35, 47, 53–54, 84–85

Incentives and motivation, 26–28, 51-52, 57, 143
Income, 14, 34, 52, 55, 57, 69–70, 82–83
Inflation, 65–67
Intelligence, 30–31

Index

Johnson, H. W., 206

Kaldor, Nicholas, 193
Kaufman, Richard, 214–15
Keynes, John Maynard, 193
Kuznet, Simon, 9, 194

Labor, cost of, 135–36
Labor force, 21–22, 76–78
Lampman, Robert J., 68–83, 202, 205
Leontief, W. W., 193
Lewis, W. Arthur, 37–38, 40, 41, 193, 196, 199, 217
Living standards, 29, 36, 49–50, 81–83
Logan, Rayford W., 199

Malthus, Thomas R., 148
Management
  and economic development, 89–99
  improving skills in, 125
  organizational considerations, 97–99
  programs for learning, 124
  and technical ability, 122–26
Managers, black, 20–21, 80, 94–97, 100, 142
Manpower
  improving skills of, 163–65
  more effective use of, 77–78, 80–81
  programs for, 76–79, 113
Marek, Kurt W., 38, 199
Marx, Karl, 148, 149, 193, 194
Monopoly capitalism, 138–39

National Advisory Commission on Civil Disorders, 55, 83

National economy
  and black economy, 11, 12
  changes in, 62–63
  growth and development of, 62–64
  and international economics, 66–67
  and underdeveloped countries, 11, 12
Needs, collective, 137, 139, 140
Neibahr, H. Richard, 41, 199
Nixon, Richard M., 127, 128
Nixon Administration, blacks in, 183–92
Nurske, Ragnar, 217

Orleans, Peter, 198
Ownership of wealth, 68–69, 107–11

Paige, Satchel, 40
Palm, Thomas, 146, 201
Parsons, Talcott, 200, 201
Pettigrew, Thomas, 25, 198
Population, black, 13–14, 31–32
Poverty, 14–16, 50–52
Powerlessness, 45–46, 52
Professional groups, black, 99
Projector, Dorothy S., 68, 202
Public Employment Program (Emergency Employment Act of 1971), 65
Purchasing power, 45–46

Racial discrimination, 11, 16–19, 59-60, 85–87, 144–45
  by craft unions, 78–79
  in federal jobs, 20–21
  institutionalized, 54–58
Rainwater, Lee, 200

Regional development organizations, 98
Ricardo, David, 147, 148, 193
Robinson, Joan, 193
Rosenstein-Rodan, P. N., 157, 216
Rostow, Walter W., 4, 156-57, 193, 194, 216
Rowan, Richard L., 205
Rubin, Lester, 205
Russell, William J., 198

Samuelson, Paul A., 194
School enrollment, 22, 26, 28, 35, 75, 76
Schumpeter, Joseph, 5, 7, 8, 9, 90-91, 150-54, 193, 194, 206, 207, 216
Seder, John, 208
Self-image, 41-45, 57-58, 59
Simpkins, Edward, 58, 202
Singer, Hans W., 155, 216, 217
Small Business Institute, 124
Stokes, Charles J., 207
Sweezy, Paul, 149, 216

Theories of development
 classical, 147-48
 derived development, 152-54
 of Harrod and Hanson, 154-55
 inapplicable to black economy, 145-47
 of Singer, 155-56
 of Rosenstein-Rodan, 157
 of Rostow, 156-57
 of Schumpeter, 150-52
 neo-Marxist, 148-50
Theibolt, Armand J., 207
Thomas, Edgar, 202
Thurow, Lester C., 50, 200, 201
Tobin, James, 23, 195, 197
Toffler, Alvin, 38, 39-40, 299

Unemployment, 17, 21, 23, 52, 64-65, 145
Upward mobility, 70, 143-45
Urban problems, 31-32, 54

Vatter, Harold C., 201
Veblen, Thorstein, 48
Viner, Jacob, 4, 193

Wallich, Henry C., 216
Warner, Lloyd W., 201
Washington, Booker T., 101, 203, 208, 209
Wealth accumulation, 86-89
Weiss, Gertrude S., 68, 202
Welfare, 70
Wharton, Clifton R., Jr., 72-73, 75, 203, 204
Whittaker, Gerald F., 203
Women
 education of, 28
 as heads of household, 15
 roles, 52-54

Flournoy A. Coles, Jr., is a professor of management, Graduate School of Management, Vanderbilt University. Additionally, he is external examiner of the School of Administration, University of Ghana, West Africa, and U.S. member of the African Association for Public Administration and Management. Before joining the Vanderbilt faculty, he was professor of economics at Fisk University; he also has taught economics at the University of Southern California, Texas Southern University, and Florida A&M University.

He received his B.A. degree at Xavier University (New Orleans) and his M.A. and Ph.D. degrees from the Wharton School, University of Pennsylvania.

Dr. Coles has served in many international development organizations and as an economist and consultant to private industry. He was a member of the board of directors of the National Business League during 1970–72 and is a member of the American Economic Association and the Southern Economic Association.

His articles on black economic development have been published in *Journal of Black Studies, Review of Black Political Economy, Vanderbilt Law Review,* and *Journal of Negro Education.* His studies on management development have appeared in *Journal of Management Studies* (University of Ghana) and in several United Nations publications.